Great Britain Has Fallen!

How to restore Britain's greatness as a nation

Wale Babatunde

New Wine Press

New Wine Press
PO Box 17
Chichester
England PO20 6YB

ISBN 1 903725 14 3

Typeset by CRB Associates, Reepham, Norfolk.
Printed in England by Clays Ltd, St Ives plc.

Contents

3

'Britain has inherited a rich spiritual and cultural heritage based on the Judaeo-Christian tradition which has underpinned our democratic institutions, laws and abiding values.

Over recent years we have seen a decline in commitments to this heritage. We have also experienced manipulation of democracy by those who would use democratic freedoms to destroy democracy itself. We have sown to the wind and are reaping the whirlwind of declining morality and increasing cynicism.

"Without a vision the people perish". There is an urgent need to recreate a vision which will preserve all that is best in our spiritual heritage and to ensure that we pass this on to our children and our children's children. This book will help to highlight the need and show the way forward.'

Caroline Cox, The Baroness Cox

'This book gives a prophetic, loving perspective on how to pray effectively for the nation.'

Julie Anderson, Prayer for the Nations

'We must listen to our brothers from Africa and their perspective on Britain today. They have at least a twofold right to be heard. Firstly, they are the sons of empire and mission who are turning their hearts towards us. And secondly, we are in desperate need of help and they want to give it. There are extra reasons as to why we should be listening to Wale Babatunde. He has poured years of his life into leadership in our nation and has proved himself a humble, loving visionary and intelligent leader.'

Roger Mitchell, Passion UK

'Pastor Wale Babatunde has issued a compelling call to the Church to rise to the occasion of today's unparalleled challenges and opportunities. His passion for God's kingdom and his pastoral compassion pulsate through the pages of this book. Pastor Babatunde is a prophetic voice to the Church. His message is provocative, but it is also a clarion word "for such a time as this". This book is important reading for those desiring a clear, biblical word in an age of misguided priorities.'

David Shibley
President, Global Advance

'Wale Babatunde has written a challenging analysis of the state of Britain from the perspective of, as he describes himself, a Nigerian missionary. It is now the time not only to sit up and take notice, but to stand up boldly and engage in the debate. No matter where we would like to see ourselves on the socially liberal: socially conservative spectrum these are issues that need to be addressed urgently by us all.'

Hugh Osgood, Senior Minister
Cornerstone Christian Centre, Bromley

'This thesis that the vibrant churches of Africa will one day be the source of renewal within the churches of the west is one that has been put forward in high and scholarly circles. Wale Babatunde brings his own perspective to bear from within the British–African scene and whether readers agree or disagree with all that he says the basic thesis is a compelling one.'

Dr Nigel Goring Wright, Principal
Spurgeon's College, London

'I hope that Wale Babatunde's outspoken book will be widely read. It is an important book for those wanting to understand the significance of the growth of the black-majority churches in Britain.'

Dr Ian Randall, Lecturer in Church History
Spurgeon's College, London

'Wale Babatunde writes an incisive message for our nation, which needs first to be read by the Church! He challenges post-modern/post-Christian paradigms which shape many of the values of our society and can also anaesthetise the Church. His book emphasises the sovereignty of God in the process of revival and gives understanding of the crucial days in which we live ... a call to passionate intercession for our nation.'

Peter Stott, UK-based Church leader
and international prophetic ministry

'By the explosive and high-tension truths, both biblical and historical, contained in this book, Pastor Wale Babatunde has given a much needed wake-up call to a materially mesmerised church, while at the same time calling Britain to her Christian foundation and the individual reader back to God. This is a serious book with no watered down gospel of self, and only those looking for True Revolution of Values (call it Revival or Reformation if you will) need read it. Well done Wale, Bravo!'

Dr *Tunde Bakare*, Apostolic Leader
Global Apostolic Impact Network (G.A.I.N.)
Founder: The Latter Rain Assembly
(End-Time Church), Lagos, Nigeria

'This treatment of historical facts concerning the fall of Great Britain is both educational and burdensome. However, it leaves us with a greater expectation of total restoration to a glory not seen before. I recommend this book to all that are concerned for Great Britain's share in the divine economy of God.'

Dr *Robert E. Smith, Sr*
Total Outreach for Christ Ministries Inc.
Little Rock, Arkansas, USA

'Many Christians and non-Christians who analyse international and national trends, contend that "Great" is no longer a true description of our country. The continuing moral malaise afflicting the nation has brought about dramatically declining standards in a nation that once enjoyed premier status. Indeed, some political analysts, economic forecasters and national church leaders have concluded that there is no remedy and that the disease is terminal.

The author is not one of these pessimists. He believes that despite the desperate state prevailing, there is hope of changing the future. He highlights the serious abandonment of moral and spiritual standards. He marshals facts and figures as he portrays the critical nature of things, and draws comparisons between the grave and gloomy present and the halcyon past. His whole thesis is based on the firm belief that the foundation and fabric of Britain's society is Christian, and that gave it stature, prestige and prosperity among the nations.

He contends that the spiritual, moral and commercial decline is directly attributable to the abandonment of this faith. He points to the Government's stance on homosexuality, abortion, anti-marriage, the Obscene Publications Amendment Act, the lax permissive attitude of television towards moral matters, the unwillingness and inability of the Church to deal with immorality and paedophile priests in its ranks as major factors in this degeneration. He also takes issue with the Royal family for its failure to give a firm moral lead to the people, and expresses sadness at the Monarch's failure to uphold vows made at the Coronation to be the Defender of the Faith. It is his firm conviction that the nation has been deceived by its politicians and betrayed by its Church.

He contends, that if things continue the way they are today, the nation is on a collision course with God. Unlike some others who have analysed the ills and woes of our nation, the author is not a prophet of gloom and doom. On the contrary, he is a prophet of hope and renewal. There is a remedy. He faithfully diagnoses the terminal nature of the sickness and then prescribes the sure and certain remedy. He passionately desires to see a revived and prosperous Great Britain.

I commend this book. May each reader join with the author in seeking a Christian Revival in our day.'

Wynne Lewis
Senior Pastor, Kensington Temple (1980–1991)
General Superintendent, Elim Pentecostal Churches UK
(1991–2000)

'This is the book for this time, written with the mind of God, the burden of a man who feels let down by the Britain he came to and with good reason! The United Kingdom, once so faithful to God, has become a harlot, legislating wickedness, and reaping a whirlwind of social evil and cultural depravity. Only national repentance will save our nation, and I pray that Wale Babatunde's work will awaken Christian people to pray and work to that end.'
Stephen Green, National Director, *Christian Voice*

'Wale Babatunde has produced an eminently worthwhile book, timely, well researched and with a prophetic ring of truth. From bishops to lay preachers, all who preach the Word of God in British churches should read this book. Through the eyes of an African Christian it brings a godly perspective on our ungodly land, but does so with grace and humility, as well as with hope for the future. I warmly commend it.'
The Revd Dr Clifford Hill, Editor, *Prophecy Today*

Dedication

David, the shepherd boy turned the king of Israel, was once accursed of pride and haughtiness by his eldest brother Eliab. His response was '...*is there not a cause?*' (1 Samuel 17:29).

This book is specially dedicated to the cause of Christ in Great Britain, hoping and believing that the revival and spiritual awakening that many have longed and prayed for, which alone will change the spiritual wilderness of this nation into a delightsome land, will not be long in manifesting.

I also dedicate this book to the soldiers of the cross – past and present. *'To those who will not give Him rest until His righteousness go forth as brightness, and salvation thereof as a lamp that burneth'* (Isaiah 62:1).

To David E. Gardner (died 10 April 2002), a prophet to this nation, called by God to challenge His people to return to the ancient paths – where Christ is Lord and King. You have been a source of great inspiration to me. The cause that you lived and died for is still very much alive! For the kingdoms of this world shall soon become the kingdom of our Lord and of His Christ and we shall reign with Him.

Acknowledgements

As the building of a nation cannot be accomplished by any single person, this work would have been impossible without the help and contributions of certain people. First I want to thank Jackie my hardworking administrator who did all the typing. I will also want to thank all my ministerial associates for giving up their time to make sure that this God-given assignment is completed.

Special thanks to my 'twin' brother Paul Slennett who supplied the key books used for this work and for the invaluable contacts you always open up. To Peter Stott, the senior pastor of The Beacon, Portsdown Community Church and all the saints under his pastoral oversight for your prayers, inspiration and encouragement when it was needed most.

I will not forget to say a big thank you to Dr David Shibley, my spiritual mentor and the man that God used to midwife this book – God bless you real good.

To all the saints in World Harvest Christian Centre both in the UK, Africa and Canada, I want to say thank you.

To George Verwer, the founder of the Operation Mobilization, I want to say thank you for your prayers, generosity and taking time out of your busy schedule to read the manuscript. Special thanks to my Pastor and Dad, Apostle Robert E. Smith for your love, prayers and the spiritual counsel you always give.

To Tim Scott, the 'Angel' that God sent to me, to do the bulk of the editorial work – your labour will not go unrewarded.

To my precious wife Precious, and my wonderful children, I really love you! Thank you for giving me the time and space to read and write.

Finally, I want to say a big thank you to You God for counting me worthy to carry out this divine assignment. It's a great privilege to serve You. Abba, Father I love You!

Disclaimer

In this book, I have drawn a number of close parallels between God's dealings with the nation of Israel and Britain. May I state emphatically that I do not believe and I do not in any way either directly or indirectly subscribe to the view that the British are the modern-day Jews. This is unscriptural and must be rejected by all Bible-believing Christians.

Introduction

'I was neither a prophet nor a prophet's son.'

(Amos 7:14)

Like Amos the shepherd and a grower of sycamore figs, I do not have any pretentious desires or lay claim to the prophetic office. I am simply a servant who has been mandated to be a voice or an echo to this nation.

Like Jonah, I have been sent by God from a foreign land to deliver a message from the heart of God to a prodigal nation called Great Britain. My message is both to the great and the small; to the government of this land and those that are governed; to the Church – both 'white' and 'black'; to the shepherds and the sheep. My message is for both the citizens of this great country and those who are sojourners.

I was born, raised and spent the greater part of my youthful life in Nigeria – a member of the Common-wealth. Great Britain without a doubt, by the grace of God, has had a significant input into every facet of my life – my family background, my education and, indeed, my faith. The Christian missionaries from Great Britain were used by God to bring the touch of light into my life, like many other people from the continent of Africa. For this I will be eternally grateful.

Right from my youth I have always desired and prayed to God to grant me the privilege of visiting and seeing at first hand some of the great centres, churches, mission houses, Bible translating centres and revival spots. I dreamt of coming to Britain, like the Queen of Sheba, to see for myself the land, the people, the monuments that still stand today as a testimony to the men that God raised up in various fields like the natural sciences, geology, medicine, printing, politics and, of course, Christianity.

My life-long prayers were answered when in 1991 I received a definite call by God to come to this nation as a missionary. On 22 July 1992 I flew into the country of my dreams – Great Britain.

However, what I met was a far cry from my expectations! Ten years on I have still not come out of my shock. Not only were the people not very friendly, I noticed that everything about the nation was money orientated! It had been given over completely to materialism! Mammon was worshipped both in low and high places. Worst of all, I noticed that the descendants of the missionaries, those who had gone almost everywhere in the globe proclaiming the salvation message of Christ, many of whom travelled thousands of miles risking their lives, with many of them dying of malaria and other tropical diseases, are simply just not interested in God and the Christian message. They are now in direct opposition to Him and His ways. The Christian laws and foundations that this nation once had have almost been destroyed, so that Britain has recently been described as a 'society of atheists' by the present archbishop, Dr Carey. Like the nation of Israel, God called and blessed Great Britain and made its name great, but like Jeshurun, she kicked against the one that made her great and lightly esteemed the Rock of her salvation.

'For the LORD's portion is his people,
Jacob his allotted inheritance.

In a desert land he found him,
in a barren and howling waste.
He shielded him and cared for him;
he guarded him as the apple of his eye,
like an eagle that stirs up its nest
and hovers over its young,
that spreads its wings to catch them
and carries them on its pinions.
The LORD alone led him;
no foreign god was with him.

He made him ride on the heights of the land
and fed him with the fruit of the fields.
He nourished him with honey from the rock,
and with oil from the flinty crag,
with curds and milk from herd and flock
and with fattened lambs and goats,
with choice rams of Bashan
and the finest ears of wheat.
You drank the foaming blood of the grape.

Jeshurun grew fat and kicked;
filled with food, he became heavy and sleek.
He abandoned the God who made him
and rejected the Rock his Saviour.'

(Deuteronomy 32:9–15)

Great Britain has rejected the God of their fathers, the God that blessed her with a good economy, with a good name and fame! The God that delivered us many times and whom we acknowledged in our national life, like at Dunkirk. The Church in Britain that used to be the leading missionary nation, a light to the nations, has spurned God's ways. God has been marginalised in many of our cathedrals and all over this nation at the moment is written 'Ichabod' – for the glory of the Lord has departed. Britain, who entered into a covenant with God through the Coronation Oath to serve the true and the living God, has again and again broken the oath. For this God has a contention against thee, O land.

It is, therefore, for this reason that I believe God has called me and brought me as a messenger to this nation, to call it back to its Christian roots; to provoke the consciences of those who are not seared already; to point out Britain's sins and transgressions; to challenge the Church to lead the nation in national repentance; to evoke the historians to go back to the archives to show us from the past what, or who, really made Great Britain **great**.

My message to this nation, like that of Jeremiah, is for us to go back to the ancient path – the path that brought peace, rest and prosperity to us all.

'This is what the LORD says:

"Stand at the crossroads and look;
ask for the ancient paths,
ask where the good way is, and walk in it,
and you will find rest for your souls." '

(Jeremiah 6:16)

However, my message, like that of Jonah and many other servants that God has sent to this nation, comes with a warning. If we refuse (starting with the Church) to repent and turn to God for healing and restoration, then we may suffer dire consequences.

Although God has not given me a specific word about what may occur to this nation, I fear that it could be something so large and great in its impact, that it will catch the attention of everyone, including those who seem impregnable.

> '"Come now, let us reason together," says the LORD.
> "Though your sins are like scarlet,
>   they shall be as white as snow;
> though they are red as crimson,
>   they shall be like wool.
> If you are willing and obedient,
>   you will eat the best from the land;
> but if you resist and rebel,
>   you will be devoured by the sword."
> For the mouth of the LORD has spoken.'
>
> (Isaiah 1:18–20)

May the Lord give us a **heart of repentance**. Amen.

Wale Babatunde

Chapter 1

The British Christian Heritage

'What advantage, then, is there in being a Jew, or what value is there in circumcision? Much in every way! First of all, they have been entrusted with the very words of God.'
(Romans 3:1–2)

'...the people of Israel. Theirs is the adoption as sons; theirs the divine glory, the covenants, the receiving of the law, the temple worship and the promises. Theirs are the patriarchs, and from them is traced the human ancestry of Christ, who is God over all, for ever praised! Amen.'
(Romans 9:4–5)

'He has done this for no other nation;
   they do not know his ways.
Praise the LORD.'
(Psalm 147:20)

The origin of Christianity in Britain

The history of this country in the last 1400–1500 years would be incomplete without mention being made of the influence that Christianity has had on society. Even today, when the fortunes of Christianity have been dwindling and waning such that only 7.5% of the population attend church services regularly (*The Tide is Running*

Out, P. Brierley, Christian Research Association, 2000) and Britain has been declared a 'society of atheists' (*Daily Telegraph*, 20 October 2000) the footprints of Christianity are almost everywhere. Christian influence touches both the believer and the atheist, educated and uneducated, rich and poor, the man and woman on the street and on the throne. You almost can't get around it, over it or under it! In some way, Christianity will almost certainly touch you.

Libby Purves, a regular contributor to *The Times* newspaper (30 November 1999), reflecting recently on the present state of Christianity and what its fortunes might be in the new millennium remarked:

> 'Even atheists should be interested, for Christianity touches everybody every day. In the past thousand years it has been by far the largest single influence on culture, institutions, law, education, and the structure of society in these islands. The *Book of Common Prayer* and the *Authorized Version* hover over our literature, our lawyers and academics are clerically robed, our law enshrines commandments (modern compensation law depends on the "neighbour principle" drawn from the second line of Moses's tablet). The Reformation, a dramatic dislocation of daily life and intimate customs, fuelled both a powerful stream of questing English intellectualism and – I suspect – the national vice of nostalgia, the dream of a past different and better, tenderer and more ornate.'

She continued,

> 'Neo-classicism would not have happened without the clerical and therefore educational bias towards the scriptural languages; in politics our House of

Commons sits in two opposing parties rather than a semicircle merely because they started out in chapel choir stalls. It has even been persuasively argued that Anglophones would never have been world leaders in pop lyrics and musicals were not that we were taught to combine tune, sense and emotion by the great 19th-century Wesley hymns and to give the result a swing by the incoming black gospel tradition. Like it or loathe it, Christianity leaves great big footprints over every aspect of national life.'

In my research for this book I came across some interesting findings, which I believe need to be preached and pondered on in an age of declining spiritual greatness by a generation whose standard of values is based more upon material utopia than upon Christian teachings.

My submission is that the foundation and very fabric of British society is completely Christian. My first amazing discovery was that this nation's contact with Christianity occurred in the very earliest times! When Winston Churchill commissioned a group of historians to find out when Christianity arrived on this island, they found their task almost impossible. Even now, no one is totally sure when Christianity came into this country.

Many people hold the view that England first came into contact with Christianity around 596–597 when Pope Gregory sent Augustine, who later became the first Archbishop of Canterbury, with a mission party to convert the English people from paganism to Christianity.

After some initial reluctance, the king of Kent, Ethelbert, was eventually converted. So successful was this missionary expedition that Christopher Howse, editor of the renowned obituaries page of the *Daily Telegraph*, in his account of 2000 years of Christianity, wrote 'on Christmas Day 597 some 10,000 people were baptised' (Christopher Howse, *2000 Years of Christianity*, 1999, SPCK London, p. 59).

But it has been discovered that long before Augustine came to introduce the Roman expression of Christianity there were practising Christians in these islands. For example, when Augustine was mandated by the Pope to consecrate twelve bishops in different places in the south of England, he found to his amazement that some bishops and abbots on the western edges of the country were already ministering. The Irish monk Columba had also started missionary work in the North of England from the island of Iona, off Scotland.

Historians have pointed to an even earlier date of contact with Christianity – to be at least at the time of the Roman conquest of these islands, around AD 43 under Claudius Caesar. Of this period historians remark that 'The Roman occupation of Britain **gave time for the Christian faith to be planted**.' They also add that 'It was within that period that there arose a British Christian church which sent its bishops to the early councils'. (Rev. David Gardner has highlighted these important points in his trilogy, *The Trumpet Sounds for Britain*, Volume 3, 1980, Christian Foundation Publications, p. 17.) For British Christians to have been able to send bishops to the early councils reveals the strength of Christianity here and the existence of some form of ecclesiastical hierarchy.

Some have even gone a step further by claiming that Christianity might have arrived in this country directly after Pentecost. Gildas, a Celtic priest, and one of the earliest historians on the conquest of Britain, claims that

Britain received the gospel in the latter part of the reign of the Emperor Tiberias. This is the same Emperor Tiberias who is mentioned in the gospel of Luke (3:1–2), who reigned from AD 14–37.

Eusebius, the famous Church historian (AD 260–340) states, 'The apostles passed beyond the ocean to the isles called the Britannic Isles' (Rev. David Gardner, *The Trumpet Sounds for Britain*, 1980, Christian Foundation Publications, p. 29). This is a remarkable observation! Again Sophronius, the Bishop of Jerusalem in 600, remarks 'Paul, doctor of the Gentiles, passed over the ocean to the island that makes a haven on the other side, **even to the lands of the Britons**, even to Ultima Thule' (*The Trumpet Sounds for Britain*, Volume 3, Rev. David Gardner, 1985, Christian Foundation Publications, p. 99). (David Gardner has done extensive research on this subject. For further reading, see volumes 1 and 2 of the same title.)

The conclusion from all this is that Britain had very early contact with Christianity, even possibly as early as Apostolic times. My personal observation is that, since God works out all things according to the counsel of His will, He would have allowed this to happen in order to fulfil a divine purpose. What a privilege this country enjoyed with God!

Israel's relationship with God

The Psalmist exclaims, *'He has done this for no other nation'* (Psalm 147:20). The nation referred to is the nation of Israel and the subject is Israel's 'special' privileged relationship with God and the benefits that Israel enjoyed as a result of this relationship.

No wonder that Paul, reflecting on the 'special position that the Jewish nation occupies', asks *'What advantage, then, is there in being a Jew?'* (Romans 3:1). He answers his own question in the next verse in the affirmative: *'Much in every way. First of all, they have been entrusted with the very words of God'* (Romans 3:2).

Further on in the book of Romans, Paul again highlights Israel's special position with God. He said:

> *'... the people of Israel. Theirs is the adoption as sons, theirs the divine glory, the covenants, the receiving of the law, the temple worship and the promises. Theirs are the patriarchs, and from them is traced the human ancestry of Christ, who is God over all, for ever praised! Amen.'*
>
> (Romans 9:4–5)

What a privilege! What love God bestowed upon the nation of Israel! Consider this for a minute – when God was going to step out of eternity into time, when divinity was going to take on humanity, He didn't come through one of the superpowers of the day. He chose a tiny, insignificant nation – Israel – to give birth to His Son! What is more, out of all the nations of the earth He called them into a special relationship, a doctrine which theologians call the doctrine of election. However, election is always two sided. First are the special privileges that come with being elected and then the responsibilities.

When God elects, it is usually for service. Thus the psalmist brings out what Israel's responsibility or ministry is meant to be in Psalm 96:3 when he says,

> *'Declare his glory among the nations,*
> *his marvellous deeds among all peoples.'*

Israel's service was to be a light to the Gentiles. They were to declare God's glory among the nations!

Again, when God called the patriarch Abraham and subsequently his descendants, His charge and commission was,

> 'I will make you into a great nation
>   and I will bless you;
> I will make your name great,
>   and you will be a blessing.
> I will bless those who bless you,
>   and whoever curses you I will curse;
> and all peoples of the earth
>   will be blessed through you.'   (Genesis 12:2–3)

Notice the emphasis – in you, or through your offspring, shall all the families of the earth be blessed!

I must reiterate that Israel occupies a unique position in God's economy, which is unparalleled. In other words, no modern state can lay claim to a similar privilege. However, I strongly believe that we can draw parallels between Israel and Britain. It is my personal opinion that Britain from its earliest times has enjoyed a 'special' privileged position with God. The more I read the Scriptures and the more I read the history of this nation, the more I come to an unreserved conclusion that it wasn't a coincidence that Britain came into contact with and embraced Christianity from its earliest times as a nation. This is something that is unparalleled among the nations. Just as with the nation of Israel, I believe God was at work here, allowing this nation to embrace Christianity and then act as the leading missionary nation through which the gospel was spread into heathen lands! How, otherwise, do we explain the fact that Britain is a Christian nation by law? Yes Britain is a Christian nation!

By this I mean this country is a Protestant nation by law! For the sake of those who are ignorant of this and for those who claim or presume Britain to be a secular state, I believe the facts needs to be put straight! England became a Protestant nation by law during the reign of Queen Elizabeth I, the same monarch who declared that,

> 'I wish I could be alive when Christ returns because I would like to be the first earthly monarch to take my crown and lay it at His feet.'
>
> (David Shibley, *Challenging Quotes for World Changers*, 1995, New Leaf Press)

Soon after Elizabeth came to the throne, England became for the first time a Protestant country by law. Thus, since her reign, every reigning monarch took the title the 'defender of the faith' and since William III they have promised on oath to 'maintain the laws of God, the true profession of the gospel and the Protestant reformed religion established by law.' This is why I feel dismayed by the recent pronouncement of the heir apparent, Prince Charles, who remarked that he would like to become the **defender of faiths**.

I wonder if he has forgotten his history. Even if he has, one of the royal historians should have informed or corrected him on his misguided statement. I wonder whether our head of state and the head of the Anglican Church, Queen Elizabeth II, should have corrected him and apologised to us! I do hope that Prince Charles is aware of the fact that by taking the title the 'defender of faiths' he will be going against an established law! Britain is a Protestant country by law, not just in private, but in public also. It should be echoed again and again in Buckingham Palace and at Westminster, for the benefit of our leaders who have forgotten their history, and for those whose secret agenda is to enthrone syncretism in our nation! I wonder how many nations on earth today have adopted Christianity by law! If this is not of God, I wonder what it is!

One thing I am certain of is that the majority of people living in this country are ignorant of what the capital letters D.G.REG.F.D. on every coin mean. The D.G. stands for Dei gratia (by the grace of God); REG, for Regina – Queen (or Rex King), and the F.D. for Defender of the faith. This is another visible and almost permanent influence that Christianity has had on our medium of exchange as all coins minted since Henry VIII have D.G.REG.F.D. on them around the sovereign's head.

The Coronation Oath

In no better place is Britain's Christian foundation demonstrated than in its adoption of the Coronation Oath. In 1688 Britain passed the Coronation Oath Act, and with this the nation entered into a covenant with God.

Two similar examples in Scripture that readily come to mind are 2 Samuel 5:3, which states:

> 'When all the elders of Israel had come to King David at Hebron, the king made a compact with them at Hebron before the LORD, and they anointed David king over Israel,'

and 2 Kings 11:17:

> 'Jehoiada then made a covenant between the LORD and the king and people that they would be the LORD's people.

He also made a covenant between the king and the people.'

Similarly, 'every monarch of this nation since Alfred the Great has acknowledged God as Sovereign over their realm, and every one since Edgar has been anointed by God to rule in the name of Christ' ('Britain in Sin', Stephen Green, *Christian Voice*).

At every coronation the Archbishop of Canterbury asks the incoming monarch:

> 'Will you to the utmost of your power maintain the laws of God, the true profession of the gospel and the Protestant reformed religion established by law, and will you preserve unto the bishops and clergy of this Realm, and to the churches committed to their charge, all such rights and privileges as by law do or shall appertain unto them, or any of them?'
>
> (D.A. Scales, *A Crowning Mercy*, 1996, The Harrison Trust, p. 7)

The King or Queen then answers, 'All this I promise to do.' Then laying their hands upon the Bible they say: 'The things which I have here before promised, I will perform and keep: So help me God.'

The Coronation Oath simply reveals how God and the Christian faith have been interwoven into the national fabric and the heart of the nation! It also shows how committed the founding fathers of this nation were to God and the Bible! If there is something that breaks my heart and gives me sorrow continually, it is the knowledge that this nation's foundation was built on Christianity and yet today we have not only turned our backs on God but we have kicked Him out of our national life.

Oh that our modern leaders would heed the counsel of the wise man Solomon:

> *'Do not move an ancient boundary stone,*
> *set up by your forefathers.'*

(Proverbs 22:28)

Christian legal system

In my search and enquiry I also made an interesting discovery, which might surprise many, but which I believe the majority of our parliamentarians have chosen to shut their eyes to – the framework of our legal system is completely Christian! Many of the laws enshrined in our statute books found their inspiration and guiding principles from the Bible!

I wonder if many of us are aware of the fact that the social security system that cares for the jobless, elderly, disabled, children and foreigners such as asylum seekers are taken from the Bible? In *Under God and the Law*, Richard O'Sullivan traces in detail the moral origins of English common law and, in doing so we are taken back as far as Roman times, showing that it was then that English law began to develop along Christian lines.

An important milestone in the development process of English law, according to Richard O'Sullivan, was around 597. Referring to the English law, he remarks 'The law of England, even in its first recorded utterances, reveals the influence of the Christian faith.' That takes us back as far as English written legal records go. 'This fact' Richard O'Sullivan remarks, 'is revealed and established in a decree issued as far back as Ethelbert of Kent and which is said to have been issued in the lifetime of Augustine'.

Henry II the Plantagenet (1154–89) also contributed immensely to the development of Christian influence on English law. Of him Winston Churchill wrote 'no man has left a deeper mark upon our laws and institutions. Henry II possessed an instinct for the problems and government of law ... his fame will live with the English Constitution and the English Common Law' (W. Churchill, *A History of the English-Speaking Peoples*, Volume 1, Cassell, p. 170)

Churchill again declared of Henry II 'That is the measure of the great King's achievement. He had laid the foundations of the English Common Law, upon which succeeding generations would build.' Of this same law, Churchill boasted, 'its main outlines were not to be altered' (*opus cit.*, p. 175). Oh that it would remain unaltered! Oh that this charge may be sounded as loud as possible in Westminster and Buckingham Palace! Oh that Tony Blair with his gay agenda would heed the counsels of the ancients! Oh that those who have made abortion available on demand and opened the floodgates for the murder of innocent babies would listen to the wise sayings of Churchill! Oh that those who introduced the Divorce Reform Act and made legalised divorce easy, and have made husbands and wives 'disposable people' and marriage no more than an agreement on paper, would take Churchill's counsel – and save an untold number of our citizens heartache!

Both lawyers and historians over the years have added their voices to the fact that the British legal system has its origins in Christianity. George Polson QC, Recorder of Exeter, delivering an address on the subject of 'The Christian content of the rule of law and its contribution to Human Rights' on 19 February 1969, summarised by declaring that 'The true basis of the English common law is Christianity, which itself was founded on older principles which are enshrined in Judaism' (Rev. D. Gardner, *The Trumpet Sounds for Britain*, Volume 2, Christian Foundation Publications, p. 29).

Not only can the Christian influence upon our legal system be seen in our statute book, but there are also several pieces of historical evidence that reveal how much this nation has relied on the Bible for its governance! It might be news to most people in Britain today, but very recently I discovered that there is a room in the Houses of Parliament called the Moses room, where there is a tapestry of Moses holding forth the tablets of stone of the Ten Commandments! I have also been reliably informed that several rooms in the Houses of Parliament have Bible inscriptions!

I wonder what all these things are doing in our Houses of Parliament if not to reveal how much we once trusted in God and His words? Again, when the new law courts were built in the Strand in the year 1873, a full-size figure of the Lord Jesus Christ was placed high above the main entrance.

The spiritual state of the United Kingdom

Apart from adopting the framework of a Christian legal system, Great Britain has also enjoyed revivals and awakenings at different turning points in its history, particularly when spiritual and moral decadence have been at their height.

One such awakening was the English Reformation, which freed England from the control of Rome and ushered in Protestant Christianity. During this period there was thick spiritual darkness over England. God's instrument for bringing light to this nation was William Tyndale, who believed that by giving every man access to the Bible darkness would be dispelled. This Oxford and Cambridge scholar eventually gave himself to the translation of the Bible from Latin into Tudor English.

So great was the influence of Tyndale's translation of the Bible on Britain's national life that within a year the king, Henry VIII, commanded that a copy of the Bible, which everybody could read and understand, be chained to the lectern of every church in the land. Parents everywhere began to teach their children the Ten Commandments in their homes. So great was the spiritual revolution in England during this period that the historian, Trevelyan, could assert:

'We talk much about Shakespeare and Shakespearean English, but our own historians proclaim that though Shakespeare may be in retrospect the greatest glory of his age, he was not in his own day its greatest influence. By the end of Elizabeth's reign, the Book of books for Englishmen was already the Bible.'
(Quoted in *The Trumpet Sounds for Britain*, Volume 1, Christian Foundation Publications, p. 57).

In many respects the moral and spiritual climate of this nation at the moment is similar to 18th-century British society, particularly prior to the Methodist revival. As the reigning monarchs were plagued with moral and spiritual decadence, so also were the ordinary people! Of this period J.C. Ryle said that these times were the darkest age that England has passed through in the last three hundred years. Anything more deplorable than the condition of the country, as to religion, morality, and high principle, he found very difficult to conceive.

Again God in His infinite love and mercy for this nation raised up the Wesley brothers and sent a Holy Ghost revival, today referred to as the Great Awakening, which brought about a complete transformation of our national life.

Of the effect of the 18th-century revival on Britain's voluntary hospital system, Sir George Newman observed that 'an unprecedented improvement in public health accompanied the progress of the Eighteenth-Century Revival', and it was due to the effect of this revival upon it that 'the splendid, voluntary hospital facilities of modern England came to be more associated with a spiritual rather than with a materialistic concept of life.' (Quoted in *The Trumpet Sounds for Britain*, Volume 1, Christian Foundation Publications, p. 85.)

J.W. Bready, commenting on the effect of the revival, wrote that 'the voluntary hospital system, which is the best known of the voluntary-humanitarian services of Britain, is but symbolic of a unique heritage of modern social service organisations, in the creation of which, nineteenth-century England led the world' (*opus cit.*, p. 85).

Wales has not been left out of the spiritual awakening, and revivals have been part of their history too, two of which were in 1859 and 1904.

The 1904 revival had such a far-reaching impact on Welsh society that bars and cinemas were closed, former prostitutes started holding Bible studies, people paid their long-standing debts and those who once selfishly wasted their money on alcohol suddenly became a great joy and support to their families. So great was the transformation that the Welsh revival brought to the people, that it was reported that Loughor, one of the Welsh towns affected, had no need to call the police because there were no crimes for two years as a result of the revival and transformation that had taken place in people's lives. Oh that God would send us this kind of revival again!

Other influences of Christianity

Apart from experiencing awakenings and producing revivalists such as George Whitefield, the Wesley brothers and Evan Roberts, this nation has raised outstanding men of God whose lives and achievements have not only blessed this nation but also the whole world. Men such as David Livingstone and William Carey, two missionary statesmen; Charles Spurgeon, the Prince of Preachers, the great Church planter and educationist; John Bunyan whose work *The Pilgrim's Progress* has touched many lives in every generation since it was written, all these came out of this land!

When it comes to the best known, most sought after hymns – hymns that inspire both men and kings – Britain gave them to the world! Which nation on earth has John Newton's 'Amazing Grace! How sweet the sound' not blessed? What comfort many have received by singing the song:

> 'Abide with me, fast falls the eventide;
> The darkness deepens, Lord, with me abide,
> When other helpers fail and comforts flee
> Help of the helpless, O abide with me.'

Untold numbers of peoples have had their missionary fervour lighted by simply hearing Isaac Watts:

'Jesus shall reign where e'er the sun
Doth his successive journeys run;
His kingdom stretch from shore to shore,
Till moons shall wax and wane no more.'

Time would fail us if we were to talk about the various scientific and medical discoveries and inventions, such as quinine, penicillin, electricity and the steam engine, which were all launched by men who were committed Christians!

I also discovered something interesting but yet heart-breaking recently about the Christian influence upon our media. For those of you who are disgusted by the horrific, violent, obscene and pornographic programmes that have characterised television broadcasting you might be shocked at this finding!

Did you know that the entrance hall of BBC's Broad-casting House embodies an inscription, which translates:

'To Almighty God. This shrine of the arts, music and literature is dedicated by the first Governors in the year of our Lord 1931, John Reith being Director General. It is their prayer that good seed sown will produce a good harvest, that everything offensive to decency and hostile to peace will be expelled, and that the nation will incline its ear to those things which are lovely, pure and of good report and thus pursue the path of wisdom and virtue.'

For those who are not conversant with the Bible, the above charge is taken from the epistle of Paul to the Philippians chapter 4:8–9. Not only does this inscription show what influence Christianity has had on our society, but it also points to the direction which Sir John Reith, the founding Director General, and his board and indeed the entire BBC were intended to follow! This inscription, I believe, also reveals the extent to which we have fallen away in our modern day broadcasting! It seems to me that those who run the BBC have become deadened to the truth and have lost all sense of decency!

I wonder what the present board makes of this inscription, in the light of the disgraceful and distasteful programmes that now fill our screens! Oh that someone would raise this in the next board meeting! Oh that God would raise a prophetic voice to challenge and confront the governing authorities on this issue! Oh that the programmes' directors would take into account 'peace' and 'purity' when they are beaming every programme! Oh that the BBC would go back to its foundations! For if the foundation be destroyed what can the righteous do?

I have gone this far to prove just one thing – Britain has a rich Christian heritage. It can be safely concluded that the foundations upon which modern Britain is built are Christian through and through. There can be no doubt that in the last one thousand years or more, Christianity has been by far the largest single influence on our society! This, I believe, has not been coincidental. God has been at work! He has always been working behind the scenes! In allowing Britain to have early contact with Christianity, to experience revivals and awakenings at periods of spiritual and moral decadence, God has showed special favour to this country. Indeed as the psalmist remarks, we in this country can safely say *'He* [God] *has done this for no other nation'* – particularly in modern times!

As a result of embracing God and Christian principles, like the nation of Israel, God blessed us by giving us great leaders, a strong and viable economy, and a system of government and education that was the envy of the world. Britain was the number one maritime power. The English language has been blessed by God and thus is the most widely spoken language in the world. We also became the leading missionary nation in the world! Once we controlled one of the largest empires the world has ever known, where the sun never set! All these blessings came to us because God called us into a special relationship and we openly acknowledged and honoured Him in our nation! It was God that made Great Britain great!

'Blessed is the nation whose God is the Lord!'
(Psalm 33:12)

Chapter 2

Great Britain
Has Fallen into Iniquity!

'Therefore God gave them over . . . '   (Romans 1:24)

'Because of this, God gave them over to shameful lusts.'
    (Romans 1:26)

'Furthermore, since they did not think it worth while to retain the knowledge of God, he gave them over to a depraved mind . . . '   (Romans 1:28)

'The wrath of God is being revealed from heaven against all the godlessness and wickedness of men who suppress the truth by their wickedness, since what may be known about God is plain to them, because God has made it plain to them. For since the creation of the world God's invisible qualities – his eternal power and divine nature – have been clearly seen, being understood from what has been made, so that men are without excuse.

For although they knew God, they neither glorified him as God nor gave thanks to him, but their thinking became futile and their foolish hearts were darkened. Although they claimed to be wise, they became fools and exchanged the glory of the immortal God for images made to look like mortal man and birds and animals and reptiles.

Therefore God gave them over in the sinful desires of their hearts to sexual impurity for the degrading of their bodies with one another. They exchanged the truth of God for a lie, and worshipped and served created things rather than the creator – who is for ever praised. Amen!

Because of this, God gave them over to shameful lusts. Even their women exchanged natural relations for unnatural ones. In the same way the men also abandoned natural relations with women and were inflamed with lust for one another. Men committed indecent acts with other men, and received in themselves the due penalty for their perversion.

Furthermore, since they did not think it worth while to retain the knowledge of God, he gave them over to a depraved mind, to do what ought not to be done. They have become filled with every kind of wickedness, evil, greed and depravity. They are full of envy, murder, strife, deceit and malice. They are gossips, slanderers, God-haters, insolent, arrogant and boastful; they invent ways of doing evil; they disobey their parents; they are senseless, faithless, heartless, ruthless. Although they know God's righteous decree that those who do such things deserve death, they not only continue to do these very things but also approve of those who practise them.'

(Romans 1:18–32)

'Hear, O heavens! Listen, O earth!
  For the Lord *has spoken:*
"I reared children and brought them up,
  but they have rebelled against me.
The ox knows his master,
  the donkey his owner's manger,
but Israel [Britain] *does not know,*
  my people do not understand."

Ah, sinful nation,
  a people loaded with guilt,
a brood of evildoers,
  children given to corruption.
They have forsaken the LORD;
  they have spurned the Holy One of Israel
  and turned their backs on him.

Why should you be beaten any more?
  Why do you persist in rebellion?
Your whole head is injured,
  your whole heart afflicted.
From the sole of your foot to the top of your head
  there is no soundness —
only wounds and bruises
  and open sores,
not cleansed or bandaged
  or soothed with oil.

Your country is desolate,
  your cities burned with fire;
your fields are being stripped by foreigners
  right before you,
  laid waste as when overthrown by strangers.
The daughter of Zion is left
  like a shelter in a vineyard,
like a hut in a field of melons,
  like a city under siege.
Unless the LORD Almighty
  had left us some survivors,
we [Britain] would have become like Sodom,
  we would have been like Gomorrah.

Hear the word of the LORD,
  you rulers of Sodom;

listen to the law of our God,
  you people of Gomorrah!
"The multitude of your sacrifices –
  what are they to me?" says the LORD.
"I have more than enough of burnt offerings,
  of rams and the fat of fattened animals;
I have no pleasure
  in the blood of bulls and lambs and goats.
When you come to appear before me,
  who has asked this of you,
  this trampling of my courts?
Stop bringing meaningless offerings!
  Your incense is detestable to me.
New Moons, Sabbaths and convocations –
  I cannot bear your evil assemblies.
Your New Moon festivals and your appointed
    feasts
  my soul hates.
They have become a burden to me;
  I am weary of bearing them.
When you spread out your hands in prayer,
  I will hide my eyes from you;
even if you offer many prayers,
  I will not listen.
Your hands are full of blood;
  wash and make yourselves clean.
Take your evil deeds
  out of my sight!
Stop doing wrong,
  learn to do right!
Seek justice,
  encourage the oppressed.
Defend the cause of the fatherless,
  plead the case of widow." '   (Isaiah 1:2–17)

'See how the faithful city
has become a harlot!
She once was full of justice;
righteousness used to dwell in her –
but now murderers!
Your silver has become dross,
your choice wine is diluted with water.
Your rulers are rebels,
companions of thieves;
they all love bribes
and chase after gifts.
They do not defend the cause of the fatherless;
the widow's case does not come before them.'

(Isaiah 1:21–23)

In Romans 1:18 and following, Paul shows how the wrath of God is at present operating among the Gentiles. He asserts *'The wrath of God is being revealed from heaven against all the godlessness and wickedness of men who suppress the truth by their wickedness'*.

The Bible is very clear in stating that the essence of sin is godlessness. It is an attempt to get rid of God and, since this is impossible, the determination to live as though one had succeeded in doing so. The wrath of God is directed primarily against the godlessness and wickedness of people who suppress the truth by their wickedness. Commenting on the godlessness and wickedness of those who suppress the truth of God, John Stott, an outstanding and well-respected Christian leader and author remarks,

'It is not just that they do wrong, though they know better. It is that they have made an *a priori* decision to live for themselves, rather than God and others, and therefore deliberately stifle any truth which challenges their self-centredness.'

(John Stott, *The Message of Romans*,
Inter-varsity Press Leicester, 1994, p. 72)

Though Gentiles have not been given the 'special revelation' of God, as the Jews have in Scripture, they nevertheless have been given knowledge of the truth about God in the creation around them.

As John Calvin, the famous 16th-century theologian, has postulated in his doctrine of natural revelation, even though Gentiles in Paul's day had no Bible to instruct them about God, yet God had taken the initiative to reveal Himself to them through the created order! In other words, nature is supposed to give us lessons about the God who created everything. So the psalmist could assert:

'The heavens declare the glory of God;
the skies proclaim the work of his hands.'

(Psalm 19:1)

Paul explains further in Romans 1:20, *'for since the creation of the world God's invisible qualities – his eternal power and divine nature – have been clearly seen, being understood from what has been made, so that men are without excuse'*. In other words, the God who is invisible has revealed Himself through His visible creation. John Stott again remarks, 'The creation is a visible disclosure of the invisible God, an intelligible disclosure of the otherwise unknown God' (*The Message of Romans*, Inter-varsity Press, Leicester, 1994, p. 73). Because of this self-disclosure through natural revelation, Paul concludes that men are without excuse.

So how is the wrath of God revealed? First, according to Paul, and also in line with biblical doctrine, there is a future day of judgement – in which God will judge all humanity. This truth finds a thread throughout the Old and New Testaments. This is not the wrath that Paul is speaking of in this passage. Secondly, Paul also speaks of God's wrath being revealed or dispensed through governing authorities, who have been appointed by God – as His agent of wrath to bring punishment on the wrong doer:

> *'He* [the governing authority of verse 1] *is God's servant, an agent of wrath to bring punishment on the wrongdoer.'*   (Romans 13:4b)

This, to me, also is not the wrath of God that Paul is speaking of, because he would pick up on that in chapter 13.

However, Paul speaks of another wrath of God, which has already been dispensed by Himself: because, even though He has revealed Himself through creation and therefore men know the truth – yet they suppress it! Since men know God but choose not to retain His knowledge in their minds, and acknowledge Him and be thankful to Him for all his goodness, God hands them over to themselves. In other words, God turns men over, hands them over! He not only withholds divine grace and then confirms people in the decision that they have made, He also turns them over to the consequences. God abandons stubborn sinners to their wilful self-centredness and the resulting process of moral and spiritual degeneration needs to be understood as a judicial act of God.

Always, when men deliberately refuse to acknowledge God through thankfulness, senselessness issues forth and senselessness eventually culminates in godlessness. It is impossible for men to turn away from God without turning to sin. A nation or an individual cannot ignore or lightly esteem God without a corresponding plunge into social and moral decadence! As Norman Bartlett so rightly observed, 'In the spiritual, as in the natural realm, decay sets in when the source of life is withdrawn' (Norman Bartlett, *Right in Romans*, Moody Press, 1953, p. 33).

Three times in Romans 1:18–32 Paul tells us that the Gentiles have made an 'exchange', turning from the truth of God and his moral requirements to their own gods and sinful ways (vv. 23, 25, 27). Also in three corresponding places Paul indicates that God's response to the Gentiles 'exchange' is that He *'gave them over'* (vv. 24, 26, 28).

I have gone this far, not because I wanted to engage in a theological discourse, but I wanted to prove just one point! **Great Britain has been given over!** Britain has committed the **great sin** – of trying not to retain the knowledge of God! Britain has tried unceasingly to suppress the truth of God! Britain, unlike the Gentile society of Paul's day, has been privileged to know the true and living God from its earliest beginnings! Britain, that was once given the privilege by God not only to know Him and also make Him known in the nations of the world, has become worse than most Gentile nations on earth today.

Britain's political leaders, such as Winston Churchill, Queen Elizabeth I, Henry II, Alfred the Great and Stanley Baldwin, once openly acknowledged God in our public life. Sadly this is no longer the case! Britain no longer glorifies God, neither is she thankful for all His blessings and goodness to her, such as our stable and buoyant economy. Rather, we attribute all of our successes to man's ingenuity.

Britain no longer worships the true and the living God – rather it now worships the creature and is thus guilty of idolatry. What other evidence do we need for us to believe that Britain is no longer a Christian country? As recently as Friday 27 October 2000, the Archbishop of Canterbury, the head of the Anglican communion in England and world wide, declared on the front page of the *Daily Telegraph* 'Britain Now "a society of atheists"'. Addressing a congregation at St Germain's Cathedral on the Isle of Man, Dr Carey, in his gloomiest spiritual portrait of the country since taking office, remarked, 'A tacit atheism prevails. Death is assumed to be the end of life, bleak though that thought is.'

He goes further to say that 'If we need hope to clutch to our breast at all it will be in such greatly scaled down forms, such as our longings for family happiness, the next holiday or personal fulfilment. Our concentration on the here and now renders thoughts of eternity irrelevant.' He further said 'modern assumptions had abandoned the Christian teaching that death is not the end but the door through which life in all its fullness comes to us.'

We must put Dr Carey's speech in perspective, as this atheistic milieu corresponds to an alarming decline in church attendance in the United Kingdom almost un-paralleled in its history. Figures show that 11.7% of the population attended church services in 1979 but by 1989 it had dropped to 9.9%. As recently as 1998, it had further plummeted to 7.5% (*The Tide is Running Out*, P. Brierley, 2000, p. 27). Such is the spiritual darkness over this nation that it is predicted that if the rate of decline continues, there could be only a small percentage in church in a generation's time – the Church could bleed to death! In his equally pessimistic view about the state of Christianity in Britain, Cardinal Murphy-O'Connor, leader of the Roman Catholic Church in England and Wales, recently remarked that Christianity is close to being 'vanquished' in Britain and no longer influences the government or people's lives. He further stated that 'Christianity as a background to people's lives and moral decisions and to the Government and to the social life of Britain has almost been vanquished' (*Daily Telegraph*, 6 September 2001).

My submission here and, indeed, in the whole of this book is that Britain has turned its back on God and on the truth about God that we know, and because God has persistently tried to win us back through different means, like raising up preachers and prophets and godly men to warn this nation, He has had to give us up! Give us over to ourselves! In other words, God has withdrawn His divine grace and restraining power and has turned us over to our stubborn ways and to its consequences. How else can we explain the depravity in our society today?

How else can we explain the alarming defiance and sexual promiscuity in our society? How else can we explain the rise of idolatry – the worship of created things rather than the Creator? How else can we explain the breakdown of the family unit and the rise of alternative family lifestyles such as single parenthood, lesbianism and homosexuality? How else can the houses of God, particularly Westminster Abbey, be profaned and desecrated by giving them over to Hindus, Buddhists, Muslims, members of the Ba'hai faith and Rastafarians to participate in multi-faith services – thereby praying to their own gods in the temple of the living God? How else shall we explain the divorce and sexual scandal in the Royal House when they should be giving Britain a lead? How else can we explain the rise in drug addiction, violent crime and murder cases?

There is only one explanation I can give – Britain has been given over! My spirit has been greatly vexed and disturbed when I see some of the sins that human beings can bring themselves so low as to commit – such as men having sexual relationships with other men, this being one of the highest manifestations of human depravity. There is only one way to explain this – men have been given over!

According to Paul, because men refused to acknowledge God, in other words because they deliberately turned their backs against God, He now gave them over – withdrew His restraining power – He gave them over to themselves and the consequences of their vain or futile ways. What are the consequences? They are primarily twofold. Firstly, 'idolatry', which is in the first of the Ten Commandments: *'You shall have no other gods before me'* (Exodus 20:3); and secondly, 'sexual impurity'. You cannot have either of these sins without the other, for each go side by side! That is why sexual orgies among the heathen nations are closely linked to idol worship. For the Scriptures record:

> *'Do not be idolaters, as some of them were; as it is written: "The people sat down to eat and drink and got up to indulge in pagan revelry."'* (1 Corinthians 10:7)

'Since they did not think it worth while to retain the knowledge of God' – because they did not want to have anything to do with God, or even bring Him into their

thinking – *'God gave them over'*, *'they worshipped and served created things rather than the Creator'* (Romans 1:25). *'Although they claimed to be wise, they became fools and exchanged the glory of the immortal God for images made to look like mortal man, birds, animals and reptiles'* (Romans 1:22–23).

Just as with the decadent Gentile nations of Paul's days, one of the most prominent and visible manifestations that Great Britain has been given over is our despicable modern-day idolatry! Who would disagree that Britain worships anything and everything except the true and living God? We have built a modern-day golden calf in the almighty pound! Who will contend with the fact that we worship money and material gratification more than the God who freely gave us all things to enjoy? Who will argue with the fact that the majority of the British population would rather go to the stadium on a Sunday to watch a football match, to the mall to shop, or watch TV than go to church to worship the God of heaven? What about idolatrous worship and practises? I believe Britain has become the modern-day Babylon, where all kinds of gods are welcomed and worshipped! What happens in Britain today would have been excused in the days when Britain was given over to Druid worship – but not today in modern Britain!

Modern Britain is a multicultural society, which has allowed a whole variety of foreign religions and practices to flourish. This has, in turn, necessitated the erection of numerous temples and groves, and has caused heathen rites and ceremonies to be practised even in public places. David E. Gardner – a man that I consider to be a watchman over this nation – shares his experience in his book *The Trumpet Sounds for Britain*, Volume 3.

'On the first occasion that I witnessed these disturbing events – during the weekend of 16 July 1972 – I had been invited by a Christian friend to attend his wedding in Yorkshire. This meant that had I gone to the North, I would have been away from London throughout the whole of that week-end. Somehow I could get no peace about going, although I did not know why at the time. So I reluctantly declined the invitation and sent my apologies. I was now free of any commitments on the Sunday, so I decided that for evening worship I would go to a church in central London. But then again, for no reason that I could have explained at that time, I set out far earlier than was necessary, and travelled by Underground as far as the Strand. It was a newsvendor in the Strand who, with considerable disgust, said, "Have you seen what they are up to, over on the square, gov'nor?" I went over to Trafalgar Square to investigate and there, to my horror, I saw that a huge shrine, mounted on wheels, had been brought to the Square, and had been drawn up alongside Nelson's column on the right hand side of the main plinth, to face in the direction of the National Gallery. This shrine was draped with brilliant red and gold drapings, and, in height, almost reached the level of the roof gutterings of the nearby buildings. Therefore it could easily be seen towering above the heads of the Sunday afternoon crowds who were gathered on the Square. In addition, smaller shrines had been set up near the lions, and three large, carved, highly-coloured, but most fearsome-looking images, had been set up along the base of the main plinth below the Column. The most grotesque and frightening-looking of these was referred to in a glossy magazine, which was being offered for sale on the Square, as 'The Deity Incarnation of The Lord'. The sheer ugliness of the image proclaimed that this was blasphemy in itself. Then, during the afternoon, a robed figure could be seen at intervals squatting on his haunches inside the large shrine.

It was obvious that a most colourful and elaborate set of heathen religion ceremonies was in progress. But what horrified and sickened me more than anything else, was to see a number of people, draped in orange robes, prostrating themselves down to the ground with their heads touching the paving stones, as they did obeisance to the solemn figure squatting in the shrine, in full view of the gathered crowds. It was appalling.

The entire scene recalled immediately to my mind the story in the book of Daniel of the crowds bowing down to the golden image which Nebuchadnezzar had set up in the Plains of Dura. The story had made a vivid impression on my mind in my Sunday-school days, but never did I imagine that I would ever see anything even approaching the same kind of thing happening here – in my own native Christian England. At that time, such a thing was not considered to be even remotely possible. Certainly, Members of Parliament and the highest in the land would have brushed the whole idea on one side as totally impossible.

Yet here was something very similar happening now, right in front of my eyes. Not on the plains of Dura, nor even on an English cinema screen in the form of a religious epic, but in Trafalgar Square, of all places.

Neither was I the only one to be appalled. One English man in the crowd was so indignant over what he saw taking place, that he exclaimed: "Have we, who once took pride in calling ourselves a *Christian* country, sunk to the level of all this?" and senior police officers on the Square had *their* feelings of disgust written all over their faces.

Furthermore, it was happening on a Sunday – *the Lord's day* – of all days! This was the day set apart for specifically *Christian* worship. If this was not a desecration of the Lord's Day, I thought, then what is?'

(*The Trumpet Sounds for Britain*, Volume 3, Christian Foundation Publications, 1985, pp. 43–45)

It is sad to report that since 1972, when the Rev. Gardner had this horrible experience in Trafalgar Square, not only has Hindu worship increased in Britain, but also this country has witnessed an unprecedented influx of foreign deities and false gods in every corner of this nation that was unknown in former ages.

Because they did not like to retain God in their knowledge, *'God gave them over in the sinful desires of their hearts to sexual impurity for the degrading of their bodies with one another'* (Romans 1:24), *'God gave them over to shameful lusts. Even their women exchanged natural relations for unnatural ones. In the same way the men also abandoned natural relations with women and were inflamed with lust for one another. Men committed indecent acts with other men, and received in themselves the due penalty for their perversion'* (Romans 1:26–27). Here Paul is speaking of gross forms of sexual perversion and immorality.

Women changing their natural sexual behaviour into that which is against nature talks about lesbianism, while men committing indecent acts with other men or doing that which is unseemly, burning in their lust one toward another, refers to homosexuality. And even as they did not like to retain God in their knowledge, God gave them over to a reprobate mind, to a perverted, twisted, immoral and totally unprincipled mind. I grew up in the nation of Nigeria, a nation that had no Christian foundations, for over 27 years, yet never did I once hear of homosexuals rising up to champion their cause! Not only is this sexual perversion accepted as an alternative and valid lifestyle in Britain, it is commonplace now to see laws passed in favour of their cause! How do we explain the recent use of the Parliament Act by Mr Tony Blair and his Labour government to lower the age of consent even when the bill had been defeated in the House of Lords? It simply shows how unrighteous, how unprincipled, how depraved the government can be! No doubt our government has been given over by God! I love homosexuals, but I will not concur as long as I live that this is an acceptable way of life. The Bible calls it an abomination! It seems to me that Britain worships sex and no longer has any sense of morality and decency – a manifestation and characteristic of a society that has been given over by God.

All you need to do today to see how depraved the British society has become is to turn your TV set on, read any daily newspaper, take a look at our billboards or just simply walk down any street! You can be sure you will see an advert with a woman half naked or nude, or a film that celebrates sexual perversion, or a story of a celebrity or political leader whose adulterous relationship has just been exposed, yet without any remorse! Consider this – one such story carried by *The Independent* of Monday, 30 October 2000, 'Lord Holme says he has no remorse over affair'. The editor reported that Lord Holme of Cheltenham insisted yesterday that he was 'not in the least remorseful' about having an affair while chairman of the Broadcasting Standards Commission. Speaking for the first time since his resignation after the exposure of the lurid details about his private life, the Liberal Democrat peer maintained his earlier unapologetic tone. He continued, 'If having affairs with attractive women is in itself disbarring people from doing anything useful in public life we would have lost a lot of our own prime ministers, several American presidents and many people who perform a useful role. So I am not in the terms of my public role in the least remorseful.' What a shameless remark! Or how do you explain the story of the 40-year-old woman reported in the *Daily Mail* of the 4 November 2000, where she was reported to have remarked, 'Now I've just had my 12th child by ten fathers, I'm ready for No. 13.'

A high percentage of what goes up on our billboards today can only be described as distasteful, disgraceful and shameful obscenity! During the summer of 2000 I became seriously concerned about the welfare of my two young children, particularly because of the obscene pictures that are displayed on our billboards in the name of advertising.

I was particularly grieved and disturbed by the misguided advert for Marks & Spencer, which my 5 and 3-year-old children described as disgusting, of a naked lady, lifting up her hands with the words 'Hallelujah'. I not only found this advert offensive and provocative to practising Christians, but I felt strongly that it was dangerous for the well-being of our society, particularly our children. In this concerned state of mind I brought this issue to the notice of the fellowship of believers I pastor. About a week afterwards my church administrator registered our displeasure to the customer services department of M & S. This was Marks & Spencer's reply:

'Thank you for your message about our "hallelujah" advertisement. I'm sorry that you've found it offensive and, as an ever-changing retailer, it certainly isn't our intention to offend or upset our customers.

The advertisement projects a positive message that women, regardless of size, are "normal". The word "hallelujah" was chosen as it was the perfect word to emulate the strength of feeling that women have shown us in response to an extensive size survey we did last year and through which we have improved the fit of all our women's clothes this autumn. Before we launched this we asked a number of customer panels, which included a cross-section of people from different backgrounds and cultures, to tell us what they honestly thought about the imagery and wording of the advertisement. Their comments were positive and, as the wording didn't offend them in any way we felt confident about the message we were trying to promote. We also contacted a number of religious groups to ensure that the tone of the word "hallelujah" didn't cause any offence.

Representatives from the Catholic media office, the Board of Deputies of British Jews and the Church of England viewed the advertisement and they were happy with the portrayal of this word. However, I realise that it's a very emotive subject for you personally and I will pass your comments on to our marketing team.

Thanks again for contacting us.'

That the best way of portraying women as being normal is to present a lady in the nude is not only degrading to women, but it reveals how far a highly respected world-wide store could stoop as to sacrifice morality for greed! That anyone including religious bodies were contacted and gave the 'go ahead' for such a distasteful advert can only be described as 'unfortunate' and it simply shows how backslidden and irrelevant the Church has become in our society! I wonder if any of the Board of Directors and decision makers of Marks & Spencer and the so-called representatives that were contacted would allow a nude lady to walk into their home, with their 5 and 3-year-olds around!

If they can't, then I can only affirm what my children said upon seeing this advert – *disgusting*!

Apart from idolatry and sexual impurity, Paul also highlights other depraved manifestations of a society given over by God.

> *'Furthermore, since they did not think it worth while to retain the knowledge of God, he gave them over to a depraved mind, to do what ought not to be done. They have become filled with every kind of wickedness, evil, greed and depravity. They are full of envy, murder, strife, deceit and malice. They are gossips, slanderers, God-haters, insolent, arrogant and boastful; they invent ways of doing evil; they disobey their parents; they are senseless, faithless, heartless, ruthless.'* (Romans 1:28–31)

Have you noticed that these vices are what characterise our society today? The fact is not only does lawlessness characterise our society – but it is increasing at an alarming rate! Why should there continue to be an increase in violence? In murder? In rape? In greed? In family breakdown? In teenage pregnancies, the highest rate in Europe? In more children being disobedient to their parents?

The simple reason is – we are living in a nation that has been given over by God! We are experiencing the consequences of turning our backs on God! The only way out is to repent, to have a change of mind, and return back to God – then He (God) will heal and restore us and send to us a time of refreshing! May this be our portion! Amen!

Chapter 3

Britain's Unrighteous Governments

'... for there is no authority except that which God has established. The authorities that exist have been established by God.'   (Romans 13:1)

In the thirteenth chapter of Romans, Paul begins a discourse on civil authorities and how believers are to respond to them. The first categorical statement that Paul makes is very important.

'Everyone must submit himself to the governing authorities, for there is no authority except that which God has established.'   (Romans 13:1)

What Paul is saying is that all civil authorities are established or appointed by God! Every civil leader receives their mandate or authority primarily from God! Paul's teaching is consistent with the whole biblical revelation.

For example the Old Testament teaching is that 'the Most High is sovereign over the kingdoms of men and gives them to anyone he wishes' (Daniel 4:17; cf vv. 25, 32), and 'by me kings reign and rulers make laws that are just; by me *princes govern, and all nobles who rule on earth'* (Proverbs 8:15, 16). It is because of the above reason that Paul calls civil rulers God's servants, agents or ministers – cf Romans 13:4, 6. However, indirectly or unconsciously, rulers have been established by God to serve His purposes on earth – to reward good and to execute judgement on those who do evil or break the law.

If rulers are therefore God's agents or ministers appointed to fulfil His bidding, then any civil leader or authority that fails in their responsibilities is not only answerable to God but they may be reprimanded, sanctioned or even removed by Him!

Any government, for example, that encourages evil through its laws or decrees, supports unrighteous and ungodly living, punishes its citizens for godly living or favours the evil is bound to receive a censure from the God of heaven – who is the Governor among the nations. King Nebuchadnezzar, for example, was a wicked and a proud king who was judged and humbled by God, not only for his wicked ways but also for failure to acknowledge God as the Sovereign over his kingdom. This was heaven's verdict against him:

> *'This is the interpretation, O king, and this is the decree the Most High has issued against my lord the king: You will be driven away from people and will live with the wild animals; you will eat grass like cattle and be drenched with dew of heaven. Seven times will pass by for you **until you acknowledge that the Most High is sovereign over the kingdoms of men and gives them to anyone he wishes.'*** (Daniel 4:24–25)

Another civil authority that was sanctioned by God was King Herod, who was eaten by worms because he tried to take for himself the glory that belonged to God (cf Acts 12:20–23). It can be seen from biblical evidence that civil rulers are accountable to God. This is even truer when a civil leader or nation professes to be Christian or linked to God! It is possible to overlook heathen leaders and nations for their unrighteous laws and actions; however it becomes more serious and disturbing if a nation's early foundations and governmental apparatus are built or founded on Christian principles and teaching.

At this point we may ask how has the British government fared in relation to enacting godly and righteous laws, rewarding the good citizens, punishing the evil and the lawless, and more specifically how has the reigning monarch kept the oath she made before God, the citizens of Great Britain and indeed the whole world? In order to do this it is important that I make a number of observations.

First, let us hear from a few public leaders of the past and see what their relationship was with the Christian God, His laws and His principles, and how these Christian values and influence contributed to good government. King Alfred the Great, for example, was credited to have remarked that 'There is only one way by which to build any kingdom, and that is on the sure and certain foundation of faith in Jesus Christ, and in Jesus Christ crucified, and it is on that foundation that I intend to build my kingdom' (quoted in David E. Gardner, *The Trumpet Sounds for Britain*, Volume 1, Christian Foundation Publications, p. 44).

Again, reflecting on the inspiration that he received from outstanding personalities who were godly men of the past, King Alfred in his rescript to the Bishop of

Worcester highlights the influence Christianity had and its positive effects on the British people.

> 'I would have you informed that it has often come into my remembrance what wise men there formerly were among the British race, and how the kings who had the government of the folk in those days obeyed God and His ministers; and they on the one hand maintained their peace and morality and their authority within their borders, while at the same time they enlarged their territory abroad; and how they prospered both in war and in wisdom ... and how foreigners came to this land for wisdom and instruction...'
>
> (Winston Churchill, *A History of the English-Speaking Peoples*, Volume 1, Cassell, London, p. 95)

Queen Victoria, for her part, commenting on the transformation that had been brought about in British society as a result of the gospel of Jesus Christ, in a message to two African chiefs remarked that 'England has become great and happy by the knowledge of the true God and Jesus Christ' (source: David E. Gardner, *The Trumpet Sounds for Britain*, Volume 1, Christian Foundation Publications, p. 97).

So powerful was the influence that Christianity had on British society by the 12th century that Winston Churchill could write,

> 'After ... years of being the encampment of an invading army and battleground of its quarrelsome officers and their descendants England became finally and for all time a coherent kingdom, based on Christianity.'
>
> (Winston Churchill, *A History of the English-Speaking Peoples*, Volume 1, Cassell, London, p. 157)

Perhaps one of the most remarkable testimonies that links Britain's greatness to God and His doctrine is the inscription on the huge memorial to William Pitt, Earl of Chatham, in the North Transcept of Westminster Abbey:

> 'During whose administration in the reigns of George II and George III, Divine Providence exalted Great Britain to an height of prosperity and glory unknown to any former age.'

I wonder if our Prime Minister and our parliamentarians have ever seen this – and if they have, do they take it to heart?

Secondly, not only is the British legal system based on the Bible (as has been discussed in a previous chapter), but the whole biblical idea of the function of these 'higher powers' as having been ordained of God used to be so much part of the British way of life and national outlook.

The Coronation Oath

It is my considered opinion that the most visible mark that Britain is a Christian nation, and that she acknowledges that civil leaders are ministers or servants of God, appointed by and therefore accountable to Him, is the Coronation Oath.

In 1688 Britain passed the Coronation Oath Act, with which she was bound to a covenant relationship with God – her government, its leaders, the Church and the people. According to this Act, the Bible was accepted as a rule book which was meant to guide the leaders and the led. By passing this Act, Britain expected God to speak into every facet of its national life. At the coronation of the British monarch, the Archbishop of Canterbury asks the incoming monarch:

> 'Will you to the utmost of your power maintain the laws of God, the true profession of the gospel and the Protestant reformed religion established by law, and will you preserve unto the bishops and clergy of this Realm, and to the churches committed to their charge, all such rights and privileges as by law do or shall appertain unto them, or any of them?'

The king or queen then answers: 'All this I promise to do.' Afterwards, they lay their hands on the Bible and declare that: 'The things which I have here before promised, I will perform and keep, so help me God.' Then they kiss the Bible.

At a point during the coronation the sovereign is presented with the Bible by leading churchmen, referring to it as 'the most valuable thing that this world affords', and also saying, 'Here is Wisdom; This is the royal Law; These are the lively oracles of God.' It is also worth mentioning that the sovereign is anointed with oil, a Christian practice, after which a sword representing the sword of the state is delivered to the officiating Archbishop, which he lays upon the altar.

The Archbishop then offers this prayer:

> 'Hear our prayers, O Lord, we beseech thee, and so direct and support thy servant Queen Elizabeth, that she may not bear the sword in vain; but may use it as the minister of God for the terror and punishment of evildoers, and for the protection and encouragement of those that do well, through Jesus Christ our Lord. Amen.'

Then the Archbishop takes the sword off the altar and delivers it into the sovereign's hands saying:

> 'Receive this kingly Sword, brought now from the altar of God ... With this sword do justice, stop the growth of iniquity, protect the holy Church of God, help and defend widows and orphans, restore the things that are gone to decay, maintain the things that are restored, punish and reform what is amiss, and confirm what is in good order: that doing these things you may be glorious in all virtue; and so faithfully serve our Lord Jesus Christ in this life, that you may reign for ever with him in the life which is to come. Amen.'

It is thus in following and keeping to this tradition that the reigning sovereign Queen Elizabeth II, at her coronation on 2 June 1953, seen on television by 27 million viewers within Britain and as much as a quarter of the world's population, made a solemn promise to 'Maintain the laws of God, the true profession of the gospel and the Protestant reformed religion established by the law.' Furthermore, she promised to 'preserve unto the bishops and clergy of this Realm, and to the churches committed to their charge, all such rights and privileges as by law do or shall appertain unto them, or any of them.'

At this point I would like to make a number of observations. Firstly, following from her promise, under oath, the monarch can be said to be a watchdog, the protector, the defender of the laws of God in the United Kingdom! If there was anyone who made sure that the government and the people of this land, followed, respected, honoured and revered God and His Laws – it was the monarch!

Secondly, following on from the Coronation Oath, the standard or measuring rod against which we are to judge or assess the success or otherwise of the ruling monarch is not the amount of assets, pomp and pageantry that it possesses or displays. Neither is it the influence that she enjoys at home and abroad, even though this is important, but it must be based primarily on the sacred promises that she made at her coronation!

Take, for example, the difficulty in reconciling these two statements: 'I will maintain the laws of God, the true profession of the gospel and the Protestant reformed religion established by the law' – Queen Elizabeth II at her coronation on 2 June 1953. And 'I would like to be the defender of faiths' – Prince Charles, heir apparent!

Hear what the Governor among the nations – the one that established the Royal House to act as His Minister in Britain – has to say: *'A household divided against itself cannot stand'* (Matthew 12:25).

The big question that occupies the minds of many of your subjects, your Majesty, as Head of the Anglican Church, is how do you feel about the statement credited to your son in light of your position and the oath you swore to? How do you feel, your Majesty, about the present spiritual state of this nation – as recently described by the Archbishop of Canterbury as being 'a society of atheists'? What are you doing to the utmost of your power in maintaining the laws of God, which are at present being reversed with your signature and being trodden under foot? What are you doing to the utmost of your power in stemming the tide when most laws being passed in Parliament today hold no standard of morality?

63

Although Parliament is now supreme and you therefore give the Royal Assent to their bills, nevertheless at your coronation you swore under oath to maintain Protestant Christianity in Britain and yet you have never protested against the desecration and abomination called multi-faith services, in which the annual Commonwealth Day service in Westminster Abbey (the very place where you took the oath) is celebrated with prayers and contributions from such religions as Hindus, Buddhists, Muslims, etc.

My submission is that any civil authority, be it an individual or a group of persons, that fails in its duty to carry out what they have been appointed by God to do has gone its own way (more especially if it swore under oath in the name of God). It loses and forfeits the pleasure and mandate from heaven and has no right to continue in power!

There are examples of the consequences in the Bible. Saul, the first king of Israel, lost his throne when he disobeyed and left the ways of God. When Solomon, despite all his wisdom, departed from the laws of God, hear what the divine decree was:

> 'So the Lord said to Solomon, "Since this is your attitude
> ... I will most certainly tear the kingdom away from you
> ... Nevertheless ... I will not do it during your lifetime. I
> will tear it out of the hand of your son."'
>
> (1 Kings 11:11–12)

Ahab, perhaps the most wicked king that ruled Israel, was also sanctioned from heaven because of his wickedness and injustice, and for not ruling according to God's ways. Hear the word of the Lord from the prophet Elijah to him:

'Go down to meet Ahab king of Israel, who rules in Samaria. He is now in Naboth's vineyard, where he has gone to take possession of it. Say to him, "This is what the LORD says: Have you not murdered a man, and seized his property?" Then say to him, "This is what the LORD says: In the place where dogs licked up Naboth's blood, dogs will lick up your blood – yes yours!"'

(1 Kings 21:18–19)

So, has God been speaking to the Royal house in Britain about His displeasure and disapproval at much of what has been going on in the Royal house lately – particularly the various compromises and the breaking of God's laws? I think so.

The separation and all the sexual scandal between the Prince and Princess of Wales, which eventually led to her death, are marks of God's displeasure! Let him that has ears, hear what the Spirit is saying!

The Houses of Parliament and the laws of God

Since in Britain, at the moment, the legislative process includes the Sovereign, the Commons and the House of Lords, it would be right to look at the two chambers and see how they have fared in relation to the laws of God! Has the British Parliament been enacting godly and righteous laws? Are they rewarding the good, and punishing the evil and lawless? Are they upholding the laws of God that made this nation great, which the ancients enacted, or have they departed from the godly foundations and precepts, which made our parliament the delight of all modern nations?

To this we will now point our searchlight. It seems to me that not only have our law makers embarked on a systematic reversal of Britain's law which was based on the Ten Commandments, but these unrighteous new laws have changed the moral and spiritual direction of Great Britain, such that we have become diametrically opposed to the commandments of God and we are now definitely on a collision course with God!

What Britain has witnessed since the 1950s could be likened to what happened to Israel in the Old Testament – in which they went far away from God and suffered dire consequences.

King Jeroboam is introduced in the Bible as one of the kings whose sins greatly provoked God to anger and thus finally led to the decline and fall of the Hebrew kingdom. Jeroboam goes down in history as the king who *'caused Israel to commit sin'* (1 Kings 15:30). Again and again throughout the books of Kings and Chronicles the writers repeat the refrain *'because of the sins Jeroboam had committed and had caused Israel to commit, and because he provoked the LORD, the God of Israel to anger'*.

This is exactly what I believe the British Parliament has been doing over the years. They have been treading in the footsteps of Jeroboam! When a nation through its Parliament legalises sin, it not only sins itself but it causes or leads its people to sin. This is what provokes God to anger!

It is true that human beings are sinful by nature, and with or without laws they would still sin. Human beings are sinful by nature, but what happens when a Parliament reverses righteous laws and legislates unrighteous laws and abominations? What it does is to remove any form of restraint which would have acted as a deterrent to sin or wickedness.

Let me explain what I mean. On many of our roads speed cameras have been installed in order to act as a deterrent or restraint to speeding and to reduce unnecessary road accidents and deaths. What happens if the government suddenly legislates to remove all speed cameras on our roads? The restraint becomes removed, so the stage is set for speeding and thus more accidents and deaths on our roads.

Once the legal system of this country was built on the foundations of the Ten Commandments. Then our families were blessed: the divorce rate was low, our society was much safer, there was dignity for human life; our children and our young ones respected and honoured their parents and the elderly. Sex before marriage was almost a taboo, teenage pregnancy was a shameful thing, and abortion was viewed seriously by society. Those were the days when Britain was governed and guided by the laws of God, when we were known worldwide as the 'people of the Book' – the Bible!

Things have, however, changed today; Britain has almost totally destroyed its biblical foundations and replaced them with secular humanism. Sin and lawlessness are daily increasing at an alarming rate, which I believe is the harvest and reward of promulgating unrighteous laws!

Let us now consider some of the laws that have taken away godly restraint from our nation and identify areas where we have disregarded or broken the Ten Commandments. After all, if by our own volition we adopted and built biblical laws into our constitution, it is simply fair today to measure our legislation against the plumb-line of the Ten Commandments.

Let's begin by looking at the emotive subject of homosexuality.

Homosexuality

It seems that in the last couple of decades there has been a determined and concerted effort by various governments not only to abolish restrictions on homosexual practice and propaganda, but they have also tried to present to us that it is an acceptable alternative lifestyle.

Immediately after Mr Major became the Prime Minister he sent out signals that he was favourably disposed towards the campaign for homosexual rights. He received the campaigner Sir Ian McKellen at Downing Street very early in his premiership, and sent a message of support to 1992's re-launch of the Tory Campaign for Homosexual Equality. Mr Major was also reported to have told friends that he believed a change of the law on consent to be inevitable (source: Home Affairs correspondent, Valerie Elliot, *Sunday Telegraph*, Sunday 21 February 1993).

Quite often our government legislates, though un-known to many in the nation, through the 'back door'! For example, a totally shocking article was published in the February 1993 issue of the magazine *Freedom Today*, and was then taken up by the *Sunday Telegraph* on 28 February in a feature article which announced in its subtitle 'The Government is backing sex education policies whose ultimate aim is to destroy the family'.

The article in *Freedom Today* referred to what was going on as a growing scandal. It said in the first place that the guidelines of the Sheffield Education Authority provided a fairly typical example of the sex education which the government wanted *all children to receive.*

Then follows a list including: eight-year-olds being told how people get AIDS, why they need condoms, and to think whether their mum or dad has AIDS. By 11 they would be told why girls are called slags and boys studs. At 12 pupils would then have to 'recognise' the right to have sex with the partner of one's choice. At 13 they progress to 'the pleasure of having sex with the partner of your choice'. The important thing becomes 'freedom to choose what you feel happy and comfortable with doing', and places to go for 'confidential' help if parents try interfering with it.

The article continued to summarise the Sheffield guide-lines to illustrate the breadth of coverage. This included teaching how to ensure a condom doesn't split and how to have oral sex if orgasmic release is all that is required. There is also coverage of what to do in case of an accident and somebody is pregnant but doesn't want to approach the authorities. Worrying the children with the idea that everyone has AIDS, at 14 there were tips on how to deal with 'accidental spillage of body fluids'. Alternatives to marriage are presented as *'valid choices'*, whilst the altern-atives to homosexuality are discrimination, prejudice, and stereotyping.

What about the Gloucester Local Education Authority? I quote direct from the *Sunday Telegraph* article:

> 'The classroom visitor from Gloucestershire Royal Hospital's Aids Department wrote the following words on the blackboard: 'bonking', 'f---ing', 'screw-ing' and 'shagging'. She then informed a 15-year-old – and the mixed class of teenagers of which he was a

member – that heterosexual couples 'have anal sex anyway', and that 50 per cent of local young people were sexually active at 16. Finally she told the group about the 'fun' condoms for young people, and showed them how to put them on – with the pupils split into pairs, one holding up two fingers.'

All these happened under the Conservative Party whose highly respected leader Winston Churchill once remarked at Blackpool that it was the policy of the Conservative Party to defend the Christian religion in the United Kingdom. I wonder what the present leadership of the Conservative Party thinks about all this. Could it be that they have lost all sense of morality? Could they still pride themselves today as a Party that defends the Christian religion, its principles and values? Have the Conservatives not left their godly heritage that their fathers built? Are they not leading the coming generation astray and, as such, a disappointment to them, their fathers and indeed the whole world? I do apologise for exposing you to some of these vulgar and unprincipled words; it is meant to inform and alert you on what is going on in our nation! Yes, it is shocking! The Church should be teaching wholesome sex education, with parental support.

What about Labour governments? How have they fared? Speaking in 1996, just before he became the Prime Minister, on BBC Radio 4's *The World at One*, Mr Blair was asked if the family unit included homosexual couples and single parents. His reply indicated his belief that the majority of single parents became single parents when their partner left them, and that there was a need to help provide the proper foundations for family life for such people. A spokesman for Mr Blair later said his vision of the family unit 'absolutely' involved single parents and homosexual couples.

Everyone today is aware of Tony Blair's New Labour agenda to lower the age of homosexual consent to 16 from their move to repeal Section 28 of the Local Government Act. For example, Jack Cunningham, the cabinet office minister, echoing Labour's stance on the issue of homosexual consent, told the annual dinner of the homosexual rights organisation, Stonewall, in June 1999, that the government had decided finally to scrap the section. He remarked that 'I cannot anticipate the content of the next Queen's speech. However I can say quite clearly that the Government believes that Section 28 serves no useful purpose, and we remain committed to repeal as soon as the parliamentary opportunity arises. Section 28 was wrong in 1987. It was wrong in 1999. And it will go.' I can report to you today that even though Tony Blair's government's bill on lowering the age of consent was defeated in the House of Lords, his unrighteous government forced it through.

That the issue of whether or not to lower the age of consent to 16 should come up for debate is in itself a disgrace! For a Parliament that was once built on Christian teachings, this is something for which we should feel ashamed! As far as I am concerned the issue should not even in the first place be that of lowering the age of consent; it should be about banning it altogether and trying to find ways of helping those caught up in this sin, frequently caused by boys being abandoned by their fathers, and needing male friendship and bonding.

Have Tony Blair, Jack Straw or Jack Cunningham ever considered the destructive effects of the homosexual lifestyle on family life and indeed our society. I wonder what view Mr Blair holds of the relationship between sex and procreation?

I wonder if Tony Blair considers the fact that there wouldn't have been any Tony Blair and all those who campaign for same sex relationships, if their parents had been of the same sex. I wonder if Mr Blair, who claims to be a Christian, reads his Bible and if he does, does he agree on what it teaches about homosexual practises? Let no one be deceived, declares the legal luminary worthy of emulation – Paul the Apostle,

> '...because of such things God's wrath comes on those who are disobedient.'   (Ephesians 5:6)

Government anti-marriage policy

There is a fierce battle raging in this country today. It is a battle that affects the very soul of our society. It is a battle to destroy the oldest institution in our society – the family. Only a few will question the fact that the greatest challenge facing our society today, and indeed our government, is that of family breakdown. The cost of family breakdown has reached such unimaginable proportions that government ministers are perplexed on how to tackle the problem.

So why is this battle raging so fiercely, one may ask? Very simple! We have a core of people in our government who are bent on promoting their anti-marriage sentiments and policies.

Commenting on the fierce battle going on in Whitehall, Melanie Phillips reports:

> 'Round three, and not yet out. Behind the scenes in Whitehall, a battle has been raging over marriage. In

the nuptial corner are Jack Straw, Paul Boateng and David Blunkett. Opposing them is the feminist hard core made up of Baroness Jay, Harriet Harman and sundry women junior ministers.

They've been slugging it out for months over whether a white paper should say that marriage is the best option for raising children. Now the Prime Minister, stepping in to break up the fight, has sided with the sisterhood. No more white paper; instead a downgraded report which won't say marriage is best but that children can be brought up successfully in other types of family.'

(*Sunday Times*, 19 November 2000)

The argument put forward by Harman and others according to the story is that 'the government shouldn't be telling people how to live'. I would have thought that our honourable Prime Minister, a married man himself and someone who no doubt knows from first-hand experience the benefits of raising children in a stable marriage, would have thrown his weight behind his pro-marriage ministers. This is a classic example of our government trying to be 'neutral' on fundamental issues that affect the fabric of our society. I'm sure our Prime Minister is aware of the fact that only 36% of the children born to cohabiting parents are still looked after by both parents, even if they eventually marry, by the time the children are 16, compared with 70% of children born to married couples (source *Sunday Times*, 19 November 2000, p. 19).

Transsexuals and Britain's changing laws

One of the clearest pieces of evidence that Britain legislates to legalise sin or what I call abomination is the new reform of existing laws regarding people who change their sex. In a recent report *The Independent* (22 January 2002) in its front page story captioned 'Transsexuals set to win right to marry' reported that 'transsexuals are to win legal recognition in Britain, ending more than half a century of discrimination against people who change sex.' According to the report, this reform of the law will clear the way for marriages among Britain's 5000 transsexuals, who have legally changed their sex but are forbidden from having their new gender recognised on their birth certificates. The report continued that last year the Court of Appeal said the government had 'failed to recognise the increasing concerns and changing attitudes across Western Europe.'

That anyone would put forward such an argument based on changing attitudes is not only disgraceful but also distasteful to any sane mind! So, would it be right for the government to change the law if some people's attitudes change towards murder? If people have problems with their sexuality I believe we should be pointing them in the right direction, where they can find help, not trying to complicate issues for them.

1959 – Obscene Publications Act

This was later amended by the Obscene Publications Amendment Act 1977 and the Broadcasting Act 1990. This Act altered a number of key issues from the original Act of 1857. The Act allows much more licence in publishing material which had been previously classified as obscene, if the contents are considered to be 'in the interests of science, literature, art or learning'.

What the Obscene Publications Act 1959 deliberately did was to make it extremely difficult, if not impossible, to convict pornographers – for anyone to secure a conviction, the publication must deprave or corrupt 'taken as a whole' and there is a defence if its publication can be argued to be in the 'public good' or 'educational'.

The effect of this act was that it removed the censorship on pornographic materials that had been known for many generations! The evil effect of this Act is that it released a flood of obscene material into our society! The porn industry today is estimated to be a billion pound industry!

Such is the relaxation of the law on obscene and porno-graphic materials that very recently Mr Whittam Smith, the son of a Church of England Canon and Britain's chief film censor, advocated that he would 'want a sex shop in every town' (front page, *Sunday Times*, 5 November 2000).

Or it might interest you to know that, in spite of the indecent and pornographic programmes we are being stuffed with on our television, the British government is a signatory to the European Convention on Transfrontier Television which states that programmes 'shall not be indecent and in particular contain pornography' (article 7). And that ... Britain is also party to the European Community Directive on Television Broadcasting Activ-ities, which says that member states shall ensure that programmes 'Do not involve pornography or gratuitous violence' and 'Do not contain any incitement to hatred on grounds of race, sex, religion or nationality' (article 22). The British government should honour the European Convention on Transfrontier Broadcasting which we voluntarily signed or simply renounce it, rather than pretend and mislead its people.

The Children Act of 1989

The introduction to the Act states that 'the child's welfare ... shall be the court's paramount consideration' and any suggestion that parents are, except in extreme circum-stances, the best judges of that is nowhere to be found. This Act even allows a Local Authority to take a child into care where the child has had a transient dispute with his/her parents. This Act also revokes centuries of British tradition by declaring unrighteously: 'The rule of law that a father is the natural guardian of his legitimate child is abolished' (Section 2.4). Is there any surprise then that we have an alarming rate of juvenile delinquency? To take a child from his/her parents because of a transient dispute is to deprive them of their God-given right to love and care from their parents!

The 1967 Abortion Act

(97% of abortions are performed on healthy babies – source: *Abortion – Matters of Death or Life*, an article on www.prolifealliance.org.uk/abortion.html)

With the 1967 Abortion Act, abortion became legal in Britain. The Abortion Act has today led virtually to abor-tion on demand by allowing abortions to be performed on certain grounds. Amendments in 1990 brought in a new upper time limit allowing most abortions to take place up to 24 weeks, but also allowing certain exceptions with no upper limit set, thus permitting legal abortions up to birth. With this Act doctors can become judges over who should live and who should die, and a mother can almost get an abortion today at any time!

Since this Act was passed restraint has been removed on sexual behaviour in this country. What has been the cumulative effect? 97% of all abortions are performed on healthy babies, and there has been an increase in physical and psychological complications due to abortion, e.g.

cervical injury, increased risk of miscarriage, increased risk of tubal pregnancy, increased risk of breast cancer and of course a decrease in fertility!

Today we have a high number of people going around with psychological scars and many of them later require counselling because of their sense of loss, anger and guilt. Many women never overcome this trauma and for the government, quite often, it means spending extra money on these cases.

Is it surprising that single women make up the largest group having abortions in England and Wales (69% in 1998)? And that conceptions outside marriage are more likely to be terminated than conceptions inside marriage? 33% in 1995 of all conceptions outside marriage resulted in abortion in England and Wales compared with 8% of all conceptions inside marriage (source: Care Factsheet, January 2000). Is it surprising that the rate of pregnancy in girls under the age of 16 continues to rise? 8.1 in every 1000 in 1995 and 8.3 in 1996? In 1986, of 147,619 legal abortions, 2894 were performed on girls under 16.

Is it surprising that abortion figures have increased steadily since the 1967 Abortion Act? There were 12,394 convictions for procuring abortion in 1959 and 147,619 legal abortions in 1986, with a total of 4.7 million abortions performed by March 1997. It is estimated that by the year 2005, Britain will have killed as many as 6 million children – the same number of Jews that Hitler killed! Some of them could have become Prime Ministers, parliamentarians, judges, successful businessmen, computer experts, ministers of religion or great sports men or women! Had the parents of Margaret Thatcher, John Major, Tony Blair and all our leaders decided to abort them, the history of Great Britain would have been different today!

The shedding of innocent blood

Let nobody be deceived, if there is one sin that will easily invoke divine judgement it is the sin of the shedding of innocent blood! God has a controversy with you, O land called Great Britain, it is the controversy that your land is filled with innocent blood. Our land is so filled with innocent blood that it has been calling to the Lord Sabaoth for revenge: How long O Lord, righteous judge, before you avenge our blood from the hands of the Prime Minister and the law makers?

King Manasseh was reputed to be one of the most wicked kings that reigned over Israel. Not only did he commit all the abominations of the heathen, whom the Lord cast out of Israel for such sins, but he was said to have shed so much innocent biood that he filled Jerusalem from one end to another with blood – see 2 Kings 21:16.

I believe our government is hypocritical! They pace around the whole world looking for Osama Bin Laden, Milosevic and other bloodthirsty tyrants in the name of crimes against humanity! While I don't support the atrocities that these men have committed, should our government not be dealing with the injustice meted out to thousands of unborn babies that we silence, even before they see the light of day?

May I categorically state that the debate should never centre around the number of weeks in which an abortion should be allowed to take place? Let's call a spade a spade – evil should be called evil and not freedom to make a choice whether to kill your child or not.

Can you imagine a man who has been cheating on his wife coming home to confess to his wife that he has decided to reduce the number of times he has been having an adulterous affair from seven to four a week? What difference would this make to any woman?

The Sunday Trading Act 1994

'Remember the Sabbath day, by keeping it holy. Six days you shall labour, and do all your work, but the seventh day is a Sabbath to the Lord your God.'

(Exodus 20:8–10)

One of the clearest ways in which Britain has defied God and His laws and has shown how much it has been given over to greed and materialism is the passing of the Sunday Trading Act. The removing of legal restrictions on Sunday as a trading day opened the way not only for the Sabbath to be desecrated but it has also had a negative effect on the fortunes of Great Britain spiritually.

According to a recent church attendance survey, church attendance in Britain is declining at an alarming rate! From an average Sunday attendance of 11.7% of the population in 1979, to 9.9% in 1989 and 7.5% in 1998 (*The Tide is Running Out*, P. Brierley, Christian Research Association, 2000) this drop in attendance should be a source of concern for any right thinking Christian. The statistics above are not simply meant to inform, but also to challenge us to ask pertinent questions. So why has church attendance been on the decline? Well it would take another book to write on this, but permit me to draw your attention to the statistics of the 1990s, which present church attendance as having deteriorated! So what caused the problem in the 1990s?

Peter Brierley, a leading statistician in the UK, has drawn our attention to at least one factor he considers to have contributed to this, the unrighteous Sunday Trading Act of 1994, passed by Margaret Thatcher, which allowed shops to open on Sundays. On this singular event, Dr Brierley comments:

> 'I believe this one Act and the consequent increased secularisation of Sunday has impacted church attendance irrevocably, and is part of the reason why Christianity may be churchless by 2010, and in that sense, could bleed to death.'
>
> (P. Brierley, *The Tide is Running Out*, Christian Research, 2000, p. 66).

To all our past and present governments who have reviewed and reversed God's law and exchanged it for unrighteous laws and abominations – hear what the judge of all the earth has to say:

> *'Woe to those who make unjust* [unrighteous] *laws . . . '*
> (Isaiah 10:1)

If the prophet Isaiah were to have been alive today in Britain, he may have put it this way – woe to our Prime Minister, woe to our parliamentarians and all our leaders who make unrighteous laws, woe to those who call evil good, and good evil. Woe to those who have removed the ancient landmarks, of which Winston Churchill said 'Its main outlines were not to be altered' (*A History of the English-Speaking Peoples*, Volume 1, Cassell, p. 175).

I totally agree with Clifford Hill, who recently wrote an article in the Christian magazine *Prophecy Today* (Volume 16 Issue 6, November/December 2000) about this nation entitled 'Reaping The Whirlwind'. Our past leaders (lawmakers) have consistently sown wickedness through their ungodly laws and this nation is presently reaping the **whirlwind**, using the words of Mr Hill.

'Those who sought to break centuries of tradition and create new patterns of family life are now reaping the bitter harvest of their folly. Jeremiah's words *"the fathers have eaten sour grapes, and the children's teeth are set on edge"* (31:29) are coming true. It is not only children who are suffering, with soaring rates of juvenile crime and more and more unruly and violent teenagers, many adults, especially teachers, probation officers, and social workers, are beginning to wilt under the stress of the social revolution. We have sown the wind and we are reaping the whirl-wind.'

May the Lord give our leaders a heart of repentance, so that they can lead this nation back on to the path of righteousness, and back to the way that our fathers trod and made our nation great! May we go back to basics!

Suggested practical action for this chapter on 'Unrighteous Government'

1. Read 1 Timothy 2:1–5 and spend about 10 minutes daily praying for our leaders. Pray for the Prime Minister and his government, and members of Parliament, that they may only enact godly laws. Pray that God will grant them wisdom from above.

2. Pray also for our Queen and the royal family, that they will lead by example. Pray that God will give the Queen the wisdom she needs in making important decisions.

3. Cultivate the habit of writing to your MP and even the Queen, congratulating them when good laws are enacted and godly decisions are taken. We should also protest when unrighteous laws, such as the lowering of the age of consent, are passed.

4. Encourage godly leaders to stand up and contest elections. I believe the more righteous persons we have in government, the better for us. Pray that God will raise God-fearing leaders.

5. Believers and churches should rise up, air their views and if needed stage peaceful protest when unrighteous laws are being considered. Remember evil will continue when righteous men refuse to act.

6. Pray that God will move in the hearts of our leaders such that they will be able to repeal all the unrighteous laws. Pray for just leaders who rule in the fear of the Lord (2 Samuel 23:3–4).

Chapter 4

The Purpose of Britain's Fall

'Again, I ask: Did they stumble so as to fall beyond recovery? Not at all! Rather, because of their transgression, salvation has come to the Gentiles to make Israel envious.'
(Romans 11:11)

'And we know that in all things God works for the good of those who love him, who have been called according to his purpose.' (Romans 8:28)

'But God chose the foolish things of the world to shame the wise; God chose the weak things of the world to shame the strong. He chose the lowly things of this world and the despised things – and the things that are not – to nullify the things that are, so that no-one may boast before him.'
(1 Corinthians 1:27–29)

I have tried to argue so far that Britain's judgement and chastening is not final and total, but restorative and redemptive! For me this is the good news! Since God is a God of purpose and objectivity, we need to ask ourselves what purpose is this chastening serving in God's economy? Before I reflect on this question, I would like to look at a parallel situation from the Bible.

'Did they stumble so as to fall beyond recovery?' Paul asked in Romans 11. Will the stumbling lead to a total fall? Is it irredeemable? If not, then what purpose is it to serve or fulfil?

Paul's answer to his own question is that Israel's fall was meant to bring about the salvation the Gentiles, *'Rather, because of their transgression, salvation has come to the Gentiles.'* Israel's temporal rejection was meant to orchestrate a Gentile mission – in which there would be an influx of Gentiles into God's Kingdom.

Paul says that Israel's transgression meant riches for the world.

> *'But if their transgression means riches for the world, and their loss means riches for the Gentiles . . . '*
> (Romans 11:12)

Their rejection is meant to bring about reconciliation of the world:

> *'For if their rejection is the reconciliation of the world . . . '*
> (Romans 11:15)

Thus Jewish refusal helped to open the way for preaching to the Gentiles – a circumstance that Paul witnessed repeatedly in his own missionary work (e.g. Acts 13:45–47; 18:6; 19:8–10; 28:24–28). For example, Luke writes in Acts 13:45–47

> *'When the Jews saw the crowds, they were filled with jealousy and talked abusively against what Paul was saying. Then Paul and Barnabas answered them boldly: "We had to speak the word of God to you first. Since you reject it and do not consider yourselves worthy of eternal*

life, we now turn to the Gentiles. For this is what the Lord has commanded us:

*'I have made you a light for the Gentiles,
that you may bring salvation to the ends of the
earth.' '' '*

'... Israel has experienced a hardening in part until the full number of the Gentiles has come in.'

(Romans 11:25b)

The mission to the Gentiles as a result of Israel's hardening was also meant to provoke Israel to jealousy. The sight of so many Gentiles entering into Israel's covenant blessings, which they would have thought belonged exclusively to them, was meant to spur Israel to jealousy. This does not mean that the Church has replaced Israel, rather that the blessings of God to the Gentiles are meant to provoke Israel to jealousy!

The covenant privileges and blessings, which they lost as a result of their pride, was to act as a wake-up call to Israel!

That we can draw a parallel between Israel's fall, and the subsequent mission to the Gentile nations, and what is happening to Great Britain cannot be doubted by any sincere person, who is conversant with the socio-political as well as the spiritual history of this once great nation.

That Britain enjoyed an unparalleled and unrivalled privileged position amongst the nations is something that I don't think anyone will call into question!

That Britain was once the leading nation as far as missionary and philanthropic enterprises, maritime strength, technological advancement and political as well as international influence was concerned is something that cannot be disputed! For example the British Empire was the largest Empire that the world has ever known! As far as I am aware, no other language has had such a far-reaching influence and impact on humanity at any time in history as the English language! Talk about discoveries – Great Britain has produced great scientific and technological discoveries that the world still enjoys today! The contributions of Britain to the world of sport, poetry and literature, printing, geology, medicine, etc. are too many to mention.

That Britain also had a moral responsibility under God (after having enjoyed these special privileges and blessings from Him) to spread the Christian gospel and other benefits of the modern age, such as education and medical technology, would only be questioned by few. However, as with Israel, Britain fell into pride and turned its back on God. What was the result or consequence? God gave them up! Because no flesh shall glory in His presence! I believe God has now set Britain aside, like Israel, and passed blessings intended for Britain to other nations. My personal belief and submission is that the great privileges, particularly the spiritual privileges, that this nation enjoyed as it became *primus inter pares* which made it a light to the nations, the carrier of the gospel to heathen nations, have been lost! The glory has departed and written all over this nation at present is **Ichabod** – for the glory of the Lord has departed!

Who can question the fact that Britain was a 'special messenger' of God in taking the good news of Jesus to foreign lands? I am a product of the British missionary enterprise in Africa, for which I will be eternally grateful! My history and that of countless numbers of people in the African continent would be incomplete without the contribution made by the missionaries from Britain. My educational foundation was completely Christian and British in orientation! I went to a Baptist primary school, a Baptist school for my A levels and my theological education was in a Baptist seminary!

What about my Christian experience? I was raised in a 'Baptist' home, my missionary fervour and passion was lighted in a Baptist church! What more? My best songs, Christian models, all come from Baptist roots – produced by Baptist soil! I practically owe everything that I am and everything I will become to God. But I will never deny the important part that Britain, particularly its missionaries, have played.

However, what can one say has now befallen the once faithful nation? Why has the British spiritual climate become a desert? Is there any visible way that we can see that the rejection of Britain is similar to that of Israel? If God's rod or instrument to provoke Israel to jealously was the Gentiles can we see any parallel situation at the moment in this nation? I am aware that historians may differ in their interpretation of history, therefore I know that some may disagree with my conclusions – but permit me to speak as one who knows in part.

I believe that the 'British pride' (and I am careful to write this) has led to God's setting Britain aside and instead raising up Christians particularly from the so-called 'underdeveloped' or 'developing world', people that were once colonised by Britain!, people that Britain thought it fit to go to their nations on 'a civilising mission'; people that, as far as human estimation is concerned, are 'the scum of the earth'. Paul, the Apostle to the Gentiles, aptly describes this generation of people that God is raising up in this way:

> *'But God chose the foolish things of the world to shame the wise; God chose the weak things of the world to shame the strong. He chose the lowly things of this world and the despised things – and the things that are not – to nullify the things that are.'* (1 Corinthians 1:27–28).

What has happened to Britain reminds me of the story that a Pastor friend shared with me some time ago on how God raised him from a humble background to become a preacher!

According to him, after he became a Christian, he began to attend services in a church near his house. Because a substantial number of people that attended the church did not understand the English language they had to translate into the local dialect.

The resident Minister was a humble but powerful man of God, who unfortunately had a very proud and arrogant person for an interpreter! This interpreter was so full of himself that not only could he not submit to leadership, but he often came to the service late – thus holding everyone to ransom!

An incident occurred in which the church had a three-day special service. As usual the interpreter held everyone to ransom by coming late! However this was to be his last! For after waiting for about 30 minutes, an unpolished, unassuming young man walked up to the Pastor and requested if he could try his best to stand in for the arrogant interpreter! To everyone's amazement, the Spirit of God anointed this young man so much that everyone including the Pastor felt the former interpreter couldn't do a better job! What was the result? The new interpreter took the job of the old and henceforth, the former began to observe the latter from the pew!

Not only did my Pastor friend replace the proud interpreter, but also God has raised him to become a major apostolic voice to the nations! Any lessons for us to learn for today? For everyone called by God there is always a replacement, in case we also become disobedient and arrogant!

I don't think there is a better way in worldly terms to describe the crop of people that God is raising up when compared with British or European standards. If we speak in worldly terms, Paul calls them *'what is foolish in the world'*, *'what is weak in the world'*, what is low and despised in the world, and the things that are not.

In the average British or European estimation, which people would we categorise as being 'foolish', 'weak', 'low' and 'despised' if not the citizens of our former colonies – I mean people from Africa, the West Indies, South America and Asia?

Are these not the people that we left our island to go and civilise? Are these not the people that we considered less than human, that we thought fit to buy, chain and use as slaves? Are these not the people that we exchanged for rum, gunpowder and other essential commodities? Are these not the people whose cultures we thought were barbaric and we replaced theirs with ours? Are these not the people that our fathers, and many of them faithful missionaries, risked their lives for, to convert from darkness and heathen worship?

Most of these folk are from our former Empire – places such as Nigeria, Ghana, Sierra Leone, Jamaica, Trinidad, etc. If I am permitted to be a bit explicit, this will drive home my point. Britain, which used to be one of the leading Christian nations in the world, has for several decades now witnessed a steady decline. First a spiritual darkness, and then moral and social decadence! Once the light on the British Isles had become darkness it was just a matter of time for moral and social decadence to follow! In order to drive home my point that the fall of Great Britain has brought about salvation to the once heathen nations, I want us to consider the latest English church attendance survey.

Using the words of the Archbishop of the Canterbury, Dr George Carey, Dr Peter Brierley, in his latest work, *The Tide Is Running Out*, summarises the present state of the Church in England in the following words: 'the British church is bleeding to death'. His conclusion stemmed from his comparative analysis of church attendance in the last twenty years. For example in 1979 about 5.4 million people in England attended church on an average Sunday. Ten years later in 1989, that number had become 4.7 million, nine years later on in 1998, that number had further declined to become 3.7 million. A 0.7 million drop in 10 years has been followed by a 1.0 million drop in 9 years; a 13% decline over 10 years and 22% decline over 9 years. Unfortunately this trend has occurred at a time when the population has been increasing from 46 million in 1979 to nearly 50 million by 1998. During the decade of evangelism the UK Church lost another 750,000 members (*UK Christian Handbook 2000/2001*, H. Wraight and P. Brierley, 2001, p. 12).

Again the traditional churches have been the ones that have suffered most from this decline! The Church of

England, for example, has witnessed the largest denominational decline in England since 1979.

The decline is 40%, or two-fifths, of the entire church decline in the country. Little wonder then that the *Sunday Times* in July 1999 reported that the future of the C of E is in the balance as attendance continues to fall.

Could one then conclude that the bleak or decreasing church attendance in England is conclusive? I don't think so. The statistics, particularly with the 'African and Afro-Caribbean' churches, present a different picture!

For example, according to the latest figures, 1 person in 8 attending church in England is from an ethnic minority. This figure will make more sense, if we realise that 88% of English church-goers in 1998 were 'white', which means that 12% came from other ethnic backgrounds. As the population of England is 94% 'white' and 6% from elsewhere, this means that in our church congregations there is double the proportion of other ethnic groups than exists generally in the country.

Again, over half of those attending church in inner London, the largest city in the UK, are from the 'ethnic minority' groups, particularly 'black'!

So what do all these figures tell us? Simple! The 'ethnic minorities' – most of whom we gave the gospel and the Bible to – on average are now more than twice as likely to attend church services than the 'whites'.

Not only is ethnic minority church attendance growing in England, the survey also reveals that the fastest growing church at the moment in the United Kingdom, is not only being led by, but is predominantly from, the ethnic minority! – a situation that neither Wesley nor Spurgeon would ever have dreamt of!

Again, while church attendance generally is on the decline in Britain and many churches have closed or are in their dying days – this is not the total picture among the so-called 'ethnic' minorities.

Another incidence that I want to point our attention to is the recent appointment of Rev. Joel Edwards as the General Director of the Evangelical Alliance! While I commend the instruments that God used in bringing this about, because I believe the Church in Great Britain has come a long way, I also believe that this singular act might be prophetic! Is God trying to say something to us in this land? Who would have thought that a Jamaican born man, a former citizen of a British colony, a descendant of one of those taken as slaves to the West Indies, would one day sit at the helm of affairs in Evangelical circles? As God once spoke through the prophet Habakkuk,

> *'I am going to do something in your days*
> *that you would not believe,*
> *even if you were told.'*　　　　　(Habakkuk 1:5)

I want to borrow from Paul's hymn of praise to God, as he concludes his review of Israel's past, present and future, when he said:

> *'Oh, the depth of the riches of the wisdom and*
> *knowledge of God!*
> *How unsearchable his judgements,*
> *and his paths beyond tracing out!*
> *"Who has known the mind of the Lord?*
> *Or who has been his counsellor?"*

"Who has ever given to God,
that God should repay him?"
For from him and through him and to him are all things.
To him be the glory for ever! Amen.'

(Romans 11:33–36)

The point I am trying to make concerns the trend revealed in the general statistics of average church attendance in Britain, and the revelation that ethnic minority attendance is growing, as also are their church plants. These facts coupled with the fact that the fastest growing church and possibly churches are from the ethnic minorities, plus the fact that the Evangelical Alliance is being led by someone from an ethnic minority – all this is not coincidence! In all these I believe God is trying to make a statement!

Provoke the people of God (the British) to jealousy – using the words of Paul! This jealousy is meant to be a wake-up call! It is meant to lead us back to the rock from which we have been hewn! It is meant to show us from what height we have fallen! It is meant to provoke us to repentance! It is meant to provoke us to action! It is meant to provoke us to humble ourselves before God and seek His face and turn from our wicked ways! I dare say it is meant to precipitate a national revival that will affect the whole of Europe.

Let him that has ears hear what the Spirit is saying!

Chapter 5

Warning to the Nations

'Do not boast over those branches.' (Romans 11:18a)

'But they were broken off because of unbelief, and you stand by faith. Do not be arrogant, but be afraid.'
(Romans 11:20)

Other renderings of this passage read:

'glory not over the branches' (American Standard Version);

'Exult not over' (The New Testament of our Lord and Saviour Jesus Christ, American Bible Union Version);

'You must not look down upon' (The New Testament: An American Translation – Edgar Goodspeed);

'do not be uplifted in pride over' (The New Testament in Basic English);

'do not be arrogant toward' (New American Standard Bible);

'don't let yourself feel superior to those former branches' (J.B. Phillips).

After Paul had set forth Jewish unbelief in the context of an unfolding plan of God for the salvation of mankind, he now uses the next couple of verses to sound a note of serious warning to the Gentiles – not to be overcome by pride or arrogance, which was the very sin that brought judgement upon the Jews! Paul uses his famous metaphor of the olive tree, where he compares the root of the tree to the patriarchs of Israel (Romans 11:18), the natural branches to the Jews, and the wild olive shoots to the Gentiles!

He says to the Gentiles – don't boast or look down on the Jews! It seems to me that the Gentile believers were beginning to be arrogant and proud! Paul is saying 'stop thinking too well of yourself! Stop the bragging. Stop being arrogant. You were simply grafted in, you weren't a natural branch!'

It reminds us of this warning given to the Corinthian Christians:

> 'So, if you think you are standing firm, be careful that you don't fall!'   (1 Corinthians 10:12)

When God calls a person it is such a great privilege! However, with every privilege goes great responsibility! And this demands great humility! When God elects or appoints a person to carry out a special assignment it's not because he or she is intrinsically better than those that they are called to serve! For example, when God called Israel into a special covenant relationship to be a kingdom of priests (Exodus 19:6), He was quick to warn them that He did this not because they were better than other nations – in fact God said they were the least among the nations! This was meant to diffuse any inflated ego that they might have!

However, along the way pride caught up with them! National pride! Not submitting to God's righteousness, but going about things their own way. This was to be their undoing! Now that the natural branches have been broken off and the Gentiles grafted in, Paul was quick to warn them not to fall into the same sin! They were to be careful in the way they related to the natural branches which had been brought low by God because of their pride!

> 'For if God did not spare the natural branches, he will not spare you either. Consider therefore the kindness and sternness of God: sternness to those who fell, but kindness to you, provided that you continue in his kindness. **Otherwise you also will be cut off.**' (Romans 11:21–22)

This appears to be serious stuff! It seems that God means business! There is no place for arrogance and disobedience! You either humble yourself or you are dealt with!

There's only room for one thing – level headedness! Gentiles are meant to learn from history, or else they will be guilty of repeating history! For those who do not learn from history are bound to repeat it!

I believe there is a strong warning to the believers that God has brought into this nation at this strategic season not to look down on the constituents that they have come to serve! God has sent us to come and serve Him by serving His Church in this momentous hour! We are, therefore, warned to be careful about our attitude, actions and utterances! We must fight against spiritual arrogance and pride!

Lessons from the mistakes of Moses

Let us learn from the folly of Moses! Moses was a great leader, a strategist, a law-giving prophet, priest and above all the meekest of all men that lived during his time!

However, he made just one grave mistake during the course of serving God's people! In chapter 20 of the book of Numbers the people of Israel came to Kadesh, where there was no water and as usual they murmured and complained against their leadership!

What was the outcome? Moses and Aaron went before the Lord and they were instructed to,

> *'Take the staff, and you and your brother Aaron gather the assembly together. Speak to that rock before their eyes and it will pour out its water. You will bring water out of the rock for the community so that they and their livestock can drink.'* (Numbers 20:8)

Compare the above instructions with what Moses and Aaron did:

> *'He* [Moses] *and Aaron gathered the assembly together in front of the rock and Moses said to them, "Listen, you rebels, must we bring you water out of this rock?" Then Moses raised his arm and struck the rock twice with his staff. Water gushed out, and the community and their livestock drank.'* (Numbers 20:10–11)

According to this passage, there were two things that Moses, the meekest of all men, did wrong! Firstly he called the people of Israel – God's people – *'rebels'*. I feel that even though Moses was called to lead the people, even though God had used him greatly to this time, he had assumed for once the position of God! To call God's people rebels was God's prerogative alone!

Secondly, he was instructed to speak to the rock, yet he struck the rock twice! As we are told the rock that he struck, which followed them, was Christ! What was God's judgement for his disobedience?

'But the LORD said to Moses and Aaron, "Because you did not trust in me enough to honour me as holy in the sight of the Israelites, you will not bring this community into the land I give them."' (Numbers 20:12)

This was very sad since this was the first and only time that Moses erred. However, we must always remember that God isn't a respecter of persons! One important lesson that I believe we must learn from this passage, apart from obeying God's instruction to the letter, is that we must be careful with our attitudes and the words we speak as we serve God's people, be it the people of Israel or God's covenant people in America, Africa, Asia or Britain. It doesn't matter how rebellious, backslidden or carnal that we think they are, we must always serve them with love, compassion and great humility! I have heard some unpleasant comments and utterances from some of our brothers and sisters in Christ that God has sent to serve Him in Britain at this strategic time. I can only conclude that they are uninspired and simply a manifestation of spiritual arrogance! For example, I once heard a remark 'The British Christians are as cold as the British weather.' Or, 'they are not as fervent or prayerful as we are!' Or, 'we are the ones holding this nation together' or 'if not for us the spiritual climate of this nation would be in chaos!' Or a pastor who, during a conversation, boasted about the 'exploits' of the so-called 'black churches' in this nation, as being the fastest growing churches! Well, my brother would do well to understand that numbers in God's economy are not always the mark of success or spiritual-ity! Too often I have heard such pastors complaining that the British government and the mainline denominations have refused or failed to acknowledge their enormous contributions to the change in the spiritual climate of this nation! My response is: let's seek the glory that comes from above!

One of the ways in which spiritual arrogance manifests itself is when we begin to compare ourselves with others, when we begin to view ourselves or what we have as more valuable or of more worth than others. Paul's remark to such spiritual arrogance is,

> 'When they measure themselves by themselves and compare themselves with themselves, they are not wise.'
> (2 Corinthians 10:12)

Christians who compare themselves with others are simply not wise! On what basis is our comparison? On the basis of our talents or gifting? Is it how long we can pray or fast? Or is it by the size of our congregation?

And we must ask – before whom do we consider ourselves as being of more worth or value? Before God or man? I believe that rather than being proud, those of us that God has sent to serve Him by serving His purposes in this nation should feel a heavy weight of responsibility for 'to him that much is given [spiritual insight, and resources] much will also be required.'

The 'I' only syndrome

We must be careful about the 'I' only syndrome that affected Elijah! In the midst of a dark spiritual climate, he complained to God that 'I am the only one left, and they are trying to kill me!' (Romans 11:3). The spirit of 'I am the only one' could be a manifestation of arrogance, ignorance or both! What was God's reply to him? I can actually imagine God telling Elijah that he had missed it this time around! That's not true! Elijah, who told you that? How did you arrive at your conclusion? God said to him *'I have reserved for myself seven thousand men who have not bowed the knee to Baal'* (Romans 11:4). So those who think that Britain is completely dry, those who think they are the ones that are responsible for the cluster of lights we have around the country, those who think everything is completely dead in the so-called traditional denominations, those who think that there is no faithful witness in Parliament, those who think that all 'British' churches are on the decline, had better think twice and repent! God says, I have reserved for Myself seven thousand that have not bowed their knee to Baal, the faithful ones! The remnant! Those who are completely sold out to Jesus! Those who are calling upon the Lord day and night to spare this land!

I strongly believe that the greatest enemy that believers from the different 'nations' must fight and conquer is pride, particularly spiritual pride! Pride is the deadly enemy that comes in unnoticed. It is one thing that can easily make us fall from grace! It is one thing that God cannot stand!

'God opposes the proud, but gives grace to the humble.'
(James 4:6b)

Recently I was reading a book, *The Final Quest* (Whitaker House, 1997, p. 53–55) in which the author Rick Joyner shared from a series of visions, dreams and prophetic utterances about the last battle between light and darkness. On the power of pride, Rick Joyner wrote:

'I was pondering how I was learning as much by descending the mountain as I had by climbing it when the noise from the battlefield drew my attention. By now there were thousands of the mighty warriors who had crossed the plain to attack the remnant of the enemy horde. The enemy was fleeing in all directions, except for the one division, Pride. Completely undetected, it had marched right up to the rear of the advancing warriors, and was about to release a hail of arrows. It was then that I noticed the mighty warriors had no armor on their backsides. They were totally exposed and vulnerable to what was about to hit them.

Wisdom then remarked, *"You have taught that there was no armor for the backside, which meant that you were vulnerable if you ran from the enemy. However, you never saw how advancing in pride also made you vulnerable."*

I could only nod in acknowledgment. It was too late to do anything, and it was almost unbearable to watch, but Wisdom said that I must. I knew that the kingdom of God was about to suffer a major defeat. I had felt sorrow before, but I had never felt this kind of sorrow.

To my amazement, when the arrows of pride struck the warriors they did not even notice. However, the enemy kept shooting. The warriors were bleeding and getting weaker fast, but they would not acknowledge it. Soon they were too weak to hold up their shields and swords; they cast them down, declaring that they no longer needed them. They started taking off their armor, saying it was not needed anymore either.

Then another enemy division appeared and moved up swiftly. It was called Strong Delusion. Its members released a hail of arrows and they all seemed to hit their mark. Just a few of the demons of delusion, who were all small and seemingly weak, led away this once great army of glorious warriors. They were taken to different prison camps, each named after a different doctrine of demons. I was astounded at how this great company of the righteous had been so easily defeated, and they still did not even know what had hit them.

I blurted out. "How could those who were so strong, who have been all the way to the top of the mountain, who have seen the Lord as they have, be so vulnerable?"

"Pride is the hardest enemy to see, and it always sneaks up behind you," Wisdom lamented. *"In some ways, those who have been to the greatest heights are in the greatest danger of falling. You must always remember that in this life you can fall at any time from any level."*

"Take heed when you think you stand, lest you fall," I replied. "How awesome these Scriptures seem to me now."

"When you think you are the least vulnerable to falling is in fact when you are the most vulnerable. Most men fall immediately after a great victory," Wisdom lamented.

"How can we keep from being attacked like this?" I asked.

"Stay close to me, inquire of the Lord before making major decisions, and keep that mantle on. Then the enemy will not be able to easily blind side you as he did those."

I looked at my mantle. It looked so plain and insignificant. I felt that it made me look more like a homeless person than a warrior. Wisdom responded as if I had been speaking out loud.

"The Lord is closer to the homeless than to kings. You only have true strength to the degree that you walk in the grace of God, and 'He gives His grace to the humble.' No evil weapon can penetrate this mantle, because nothing can overpower His grace. As long as you wear this mantle you are safe from this kind of attack." '

Chapter 6

The Prodigal Church in a Prodigal World

'Now you, if you call yourself a Jew; if you rely on the law and brag about your relationship to God; if you know his will and approve of what is superior because you are instructed by the law; if you are convinced that you are a guide for the blind, a light for those who are in the dark, an instructor of the foolish, a teacher of infants, because you have in the law the embodiment of knowledge and truth – you, then, who teach others, do you not teach yourself? You who preach against stealing, do you steal? You who say that people should not commit adultery, do you commit adultery? You who abhor idols, do you rob temples? You who brag about the law, do you dishonour God by breaking the law? As it is written: "God's name is blasphemed among the Gentiles because of you." '

(Romans 2:17–24)

'For it is time for judgement to begin with the family of God . . . ' (1 Peter 4:17 NASB)

Great Britain has fallen morally and spiritually because the Church has fallen. Great Britain is backslidden. The nation is prodigal because the Church is prodigal. God has been kicked out of much of Great Britain because God is no longer in many of our churches. He has long been shown the way out of His own Church and there is a signboard in front of our cathedrals 'Out of bounds, please keep out'. The truth has been lost in the streets of Great Britain, because the truth has been lost in the Church. There is evil and sin in this nation, because there is sin in the camp of God's people.

The account of man's fall and God's interrogation reveals something fundamental about human nature. We always look for someone else we can blame for our failures and shortcomings. After eating the forbidden fruit and being questioned by God, Adam's reply was *'The woman you put here with me – she gave me some fruit from the tree, and I ate it'* (Genesis 3:12). The blame for his disobedience was passed onto the woman. What about Eve? Was she going to take responsibility for her failure? Far from it! Her reply was *'The serpent deceived me, and I ate'* (Genesis 3:13b). This is typical of all human beings. We always want to pass the blame to someone else. So who do we blame for Britain's present moral and spiritual decline?

Who is to blame for almost 5 million legal abortions that have been carried out since 1967? Who is to blame for Britain having the highest rate of divorce and teenage pregnancy in Europe? Who is to blame for the loss of morality in our national life where there are no longer moral absolutes? Who is to blame today, where alternative sexual lifestyles such as homosexuality and lesbianism have been accepted as valid lifestyles instead of the traditional family relationships? Quite often when we tune into our TV sets, read the newspapers or simply get involved in a conversation about the deplorable state of the nation, it is quite common to blame the Prime

Minister and his government and many of the parastatal groups or establishments. While this may be true, however, the truth is that the blame for the moral and spiritual state of the nation should be laid at the doorstep of the Church. As it goes in the Church, so it is in the nation. Society throughout human history has always reflected the state of the Church. Whenever the Church has been revived, it has always affected society. After all, the Church has been called by God to not only affect and impact society, but to be an example to them.

Called to be salt and light

In the Matthew 5:13–16, Jesus states the role His followers or believers are meant to be playing in their society, salt and light.

> 'You are the salt of the earth. But if the salt loses its saltiness, how can it be made salty again? It is no longer good for anything, except to be thrown out and trampled by men. You are the light of the world. A city on a hill cannot be hidden. Neither do people light a lamp and put it under a bowl. Instead they put on its stand, and it gives light to everyone in the house. In the same way let your light shine before men, that they may see your good deeds and praise your Father in heaven.'

Christians are supposed to play the same role as salt and light in our home. Christians, like salt, are supposed to be the preserving factor in society. As light, we are supposed to dispel darkness or evil. We are to stand up for what is right and refuse what is evil. However, if we are not fulfilling our purpose in society Jesus said we are good for nothing, useless – and there is only one thing remaining for us, be thrown out and trampled by men.

How the Bible views those outside Christ

The Bible uses various words and phrases to describe individuals who do not have a personal relationship with Christ, in other words those that are not committed Christians. The Bible describes such people as being lost, dead in sin, blind, enemies of God, those whose names are not written in the book of life, those in darkness, etc. Because sinners are in such a pathetic state spiritually, Christians have been called by God to witness to these people through their lives and their words. So Christians who are supposed to be in the light are meant to lead people out of darkness.

So what happens if the supposed children of light are riddled with the same sin as the children of darkness? Jesus likens this to a 'blind man trying to lead the blind.' So how can a Church that is filled with and taken over by iniquity be a witness to a backslidden and prodigal society? I think this is impossible.

The Church in Great Britain at this moment could at best be described as blind, bankrupt, cold, frozen, worldly, compromising and dead. Many of our denominations today, rather than being a movement, have become a monument that attracts more tourists than sinners or even worshippers. I believe Revelation 3:20 is really applicable to the Church in Britain. It is a plea by the risen Lord to be allowed entrance into His Church. *'Behold! I stand at the door and knock.'* Unfortunately many of our Christian leaders cannot hear the sound of His knock or, better put, have hardened their hearts.

Many Bible scholars believe, and I agree, that the Church of today is in the Laodicean age. It has become a Church that is miserable, a Church that suffers from self-deception and is spiritually anaemic, a Church that thinks it is rich, full and without need of anything.

> 'To the angel of the church in Laodicea write: These are the words of the Amen, the faithful and true witness, the ruler of God's creation. I know your deeds, that you are neither cold nor hot. I wish you were either one or the other! So, because you are lukewarm – neither hot nor cold – I am about to spit you out of my mouth. You say, "I am rich; I have acquired wealth, and do not need a thing." But you do not realise that you are wretched, pitiful, poor, blind and naked. I counsel you to buy from me gold refined in the fire, so that you can become rich; and white clothes to wear, so that you can cover your shameful nakedness, and salve to put on your eyes, so that you can see.'
>
> (Revelation 3:14–18)

Our Bible colleges and theological seminaries

Many of the lecturers in our Bible colleges and seminaries today are people who do not hold a firm and uncompromising belief in some of the fundamentals of the Christian faith. It is thus a bunch of dead lecturers, passing on a dead message, producing a bunch of dead ministers. This accounts today for the large number of priests and clergy who hold on to liberal doctrines. As one of our spiritual forefathers, Leonard Ravenhill, has affirmed,

> 'Christ is now "wounded in the house of His friends". The Holy Book of the living God suffers more from its exponents today than from its opponents.'
>
> (*Why Revival Tarries*, Leonard Ravenhill,
Sovereign World, 1959, p. 82)

Josh McDowell and Bob Hostetler, co-authors of the book *The New Tolerance* (Tyndale House, 1998, p. 175), share the story of a dean of a mainline divinity school who went to speak at Steve's (a Canadian pastor's) seminary class on apologetics. The visiting professor shared about his journey from evangelical apologetics professor to self-proclaimed atheist. Steve wrote:

> 'He also shared ... his belief that each culture develops [its] own reality or truth. He stated that, just as Santa Claus doesn't need to be real to have an effect, so different religions or beliefs are equally real regardless of their foundation in truth or fact.
>
> As the time for questions began ... I asked the visitor, "Do you believe there is an absolute moral truth?" Although a long answer was given, the answer was "no", and he returned to his argument that "each culture and even subculture determines [its] own reality or truth".
>
> I then asked him, "If there is no absolute truth, does that mean that what Hitler did was right in his culture but wrong in our culture?"'

So, do I think the college professor is wrong? I think absolutely so. Is this an isolated case? I don't think so; the professor simply reflects what our theological seminaries have been turned into by liberal theologians who have been given up by God, and who do not have a right to speak on behalf of a God who is foreign to them. In the words of Jesus, they are blind guides, the blind leading the blind. The outcome is ultimately the pit. Little wonder that many Bible practising believers run away from many of these seminaries, because they are more of a theological cemetery than a seminary.

Love, sex, marriage and the Church

I think there's an area where the Church has compromised and suffered great assault in Britain today: the area of sex, love and marriage. While I was growing up, premarital sex and cohabitation was a thing of shame. Those who had sex outside marriage and cohabited not only broke God's law but they brought shame and dishonour to their families. Pregnancy outside marriage was disapproved of strongly in society, whilst separation and divorce were almost taboo. I gather it was the same in this country some decades ago. However the Church has taken a soft stance on cohabitation and sex before marriage.

In fact, in my own judgement, the Church is simply reflecting society on this issue. The percentage of people cohabiting and having sex before marriage is now reaching alarming proportions. The Church, to our shame, has become more and more permissive or blind to sex before marriage and cohabitation, so that anyone who stands for the opposite is viewed as being old fashioned.

As recently as 1997 a poll that was taken by a church research group reported that 'A quarter of teenagers who go to church have taken part in sexual activity by the time they are 15. Fifteen percent have had full intercourse' (quoted from the pamphlet *Britain in Sin* by The Christian Voice, p. 30).

The Church and paedophile priests

I have seen an evil under the sun – supposed representatives and priests of God sexually abusing children. This is not only heart-breaking but disgraceful. In a shameful article in the *Daily Mail* of the 13 September 2000, the MPs' watchdog was called in to target paedophile priests.

Can you imagine this? The priests who are meant to teach and correct society's morals are the ones being told how to behave by the government. In the same article, it was reported that a plea to help the Roman Catholic Church rid itself of paedophile priests was made to parliamentary 'sleaze buster' Lord Nolan the previous day. The article reported that a particular Bishop had been appointed by his Archbishop, even though his boss knew of his paedophile activities, and more abuse followed.

The report stated furthermore that in the last five years 21 Catholic priests (more than one in every 300 in England and Wales), have been convicted of sex offences against children including altar boys and servers, sometimes in churches.

I wonder what our prayer should be for those abusing innocent children? Should we pray that God should deliver these priests from this immoral and shameful behaviour or should we pray that God should deliver our children from the so-called priests that are ordained to serve them?

The Church and homosexuality

In no other area has the Church been so divided and compromised, received such bad press and indeed disappointed God than in the emotive subject of homosexuality. May I say that as Christians we have been called to love sinners and pray for them, but nowhere are we called in the Bible to love sin. Nowhere are we called in the Bible to compromise God's standard. Nowhere are we told in the Bible that God's moral standard changes with time. May I state categorically that same sex sexual relationships in the Bible are considered as sin or sodomy.

In Ezekiel we are told the reason why the twin cities of Sodom and Gomorrah were destroyed.

> 'Now this was the sin of your sister Sodom: She and her daughters were arrogant, overfed and unconcerned; they did not help the poor and needy. They were haughty and did detestable things before me.'   (Ezekiel 16:49–50)

The above scripture summarises the reasons for the destruction of Sodom as pride, an overabundance of food, prosperous ease, neglect of the poor and of course they did detestable things or abominable acts.

I am aware that Bible scholars and interpreters are divided regarding the reason for the destruction of Sodom and Gomorrah. However, it is obvious to me, at least from this scripture and Genesis chapter 19, that one of the reasons why they were destroyed was because of their detestable acts or what other translations call 'abominations'.

Unger's Bible Dictionary (Moody Press, p. 9) defines the word as that 'which is particularly offensive to the moral sense, the religious feeling, or the natural inclination of the soul'. I personally believe that the abominable or detestable acts mentioned in Ezekiel 16:49–50 fit very much into the account of Genesis 19. My submission is that one of the key reasons for Sodom's destruction was the homosexual practices of the Sodomites.

In Romans 1:24–32 speaking about the decadent Gentile world of his days, Paul spoke against homosexuality and lesbianism as sins that are not only a manifestation of a depraved and unprincipled mind, but they invite divine judgement for those who practise such acts. I am aware of the many arguments that people put forward for practising same sex relationships, such as the fact that they were created with this condition. Some have even argued that it is a medical condition. Nothing could be further from the truth. I do know from my knowledge of Scripture that when God instituted marriage it was between Adam and Eve and not Adam and Steve.

Sex in marriage was not only meant to celebrate mutual love, but it was meant to lead to procreation – the procreation of mankind. I have often wondered if practising homosexuals and their supporters know that it would have been impossible for them to come into this world if their parents were the same sex.

So how has the Church fared on this divisive subject plaguing our society? As recently as 1996 the spiritual leader of the Anglican Church, Most Reverend George L. Carey, visited Los Angeles and commented on the ordination of homosexuals. He remarked that homosexuals should not be ordained unless 'the vast majority' of Church members support the move. 'Be careful,' he said, 'that we do not run into making rash decisions that can deeply divide the church and weaken its effectiveness' (*The Los Angeles Times*, 25 May 1996).

The above attitude to the issue of the ordination of homosexuals is very typical of British spiritual leaders. I wonder if Dr Carey thinks that the 'majority' is always right, or does he think that biblical morality is based on consensus? God's moral standards are absolute, and His Word is not a respecter of persons including the majority. I wonder if the Archbishop remembers the admonition from the Scriptures that we should not follow the multitudes to do evil. Does the Archbishop believe that the Scriptures and not the majority have the final authority on the matter of doctrine and practise? We should remember Jesus' rebuke to the spiritual elites and hypocrites of His day, those who made the Word of God void by clinging to human traditions! I think that like Archbishop Carey many church leaders and Christians are more concerned about the 'unity' and the 'reputation' (if there is any) of the Church in the eyes of the public than in standing with other great reformers who risked and gave their lives for the truth of the Scriptures. In any event I don't think the Anglican Church can be more divided and more weakened than it is today. Let's remember that it is not our responsibility to build the Church – Jesus will do that. Ours is simply to stay faithful and true to the faith that was once delivered to the saints.

Modernisation or sin?

One of the commonest accusations laid at the doorstep of the Church today is that we are not moving on with the times. In other words we must be responding to the changes in every generation. While this may be valid when it comes to our method, I do not believe that we should ever change our message, particularly the content, to suit the carnal cravings of a backslidden society. I believe that in trying to be relevant to an ever-changing society, the Church in this country has lost and compromised its message. For example as recently as October 2000, Michael Doe, the Bishop of Swindon, called on the Church of England to modernise by holding blessings for homosexual couples. Michael Doe in his report said that it was no longer possible to pretend that marriage was better than gay relationships because 'the world has moved on'. He insisted further that sanctifying gay couples would buttress traditional marriage by showing how the Church valued committed relationships. The Bishop went on to state that: 'We can no longer pretend that there is "marriage" and there is "sodomy", the world has moved on and the church needs to move on as well' (*Daily Mail* 9 October 2000).

I wonder what kind of Bible Bishop Doe reads? I also wonder if he thinks that God's morality changes with every age? Very soon, I think some of our bishops will be canvassing for the Church to accept and ordain those who take other people's wives and husbands because the world approves of it. We are called to be separate from the world and not to conform to the world system.

> '*Do not conform any longer to the pattern of this world, but be transformed by the renewing of your mind.*'
> (Romans 12:2)

In the same article, he was reported to have insisted that 'gay relationships may be acceptable among the laity, but never among the clergy; and that sex should be reserved for marriage' (*Daily Mail*, 9 October 2000). Again, I wonder whether this is not a double standard? Are we saying that gay relationships are right for the laity and wrong for the clergy? I am not aware of any scripture as far as morality is concerned that allows the laity to behave in a certain way, but disallows the clergy from behaving in the same way. I believe that what applies to the leaders also applies to the led. I think we should face the truth, rather than finding a middle ground. Evil in Scripture is called evil and we are challenged to repent or else we will perish!

Church online with gay weddings

As I was researching this book I came across a shocking find – a Scottish church has gone on the Internet to advertise homosexual, bisexual and transgender weddings.

In their web page, the Holy Trinity Metropolitan Community Church in Edinburgh, the first in Scotland to offer
religious blessings to same-sex couples says, 'We offer
relationship blessings to couples irrespective of gender
identification or sexuality.' The treasurer of the church
says: 'We request that people go to counselling and that
they attend two services at the church before the blessing.'
The church advert went on to state that the church wants
to see homosexual marriages legalised in Britain, as they
are in Denmark (*Daily Telegraph*, Monday, 8 June 1998).
Not only is the church blessing same sex 'marriage', but
also they are canvassing for it to become legal. What a
manifestation and demonstration of an unprincipled
mind! We have in so doing done damage to the Scriptures.
I wonder how many gay marriages Jesus or the apostles
blessed? I submit to the Church of Great Britain that
unless we repent, the judgement of God will fall on this
nation. In fact Sodom and Gomorrah's sins were not
greater than ours, yet they were totally destroyed. I know
that I will be treading upon many toes; I know that some
of my readers may consider me an extremist, but I can
either choose to follow many of our spiritual leaders who
know the truth and yet keep quiet, or be true to my
conscience and what I consider to be the truth of God's
Word. May God deliver us from the fear of men, and
worldly fame and popularity, and help us seek that which
comes from above.

The 'peace and prosperity' preachers

There is an evil that I have seen in the Church of Christ
today – it is the evil of the so-called 'peace and prosperity'
preachers, preachers that are out to please men and not
God. I am privileged to listen to and read materials from

many ministers today. I believe some are doing more damage than good to the cause of Christ. They are promising peace, when the Prince of Peace says there is no peace for the unrighteous. I believe many of our preachers today – and I suspect that a lot of it was exported from America – are not balanced in their message. A lot of messages that we hear today are centred on prosperity, material and physical. Yet only few ever preach on repentance, the cross of Christ, sacrifice, holiness, the second coming, heaven and hell. Before you judge me, let me state categorically to you that I believe that the message of prosperity is biblical. God's will is to prosper us, bless our family and everything that we lay our hands upon, based on obeying His Word fully. 3 John 2, which is my favourite passage, speaks not just of physical and material prosperity but also that of the soul.

> *'Dear friend, I pray that you may enjoy good health and that all may go well with you, even as your soul is getting along well.'*

Any prosperity that does not include the prosperity of the soul is not complete. While we are grateful to God for the breakthroughs that he is giving to the Church at this hour, I however believe that the Church needs more messages on revival, holiness, sacrifice, the great commission and messages on how to transform this society. I believe the West has too many material possessions, and that to ask God for more will amount for many to greed.

I think many of us today don't need faith to have the basic necessities of life in this country – we have more than enough. However, we do need faith to take this land; we need more messages that will send us to our knees in prayer, we need messages that will challenge us to fight for the rights of the poor, the widows and the fatherless. We need messages on the one new man that eliminates all forms of erroneous distinctions in the Body of Christ. While I am not painting a picture of despair, we must face up to reality. We cannot be shouting 'peace, peace', when the whole nation around us is on fire! This nation needs rescuers; this nation needs prophets like Elijah and John the Baptist, who will be bold enough to call the Church and the nation to repentance. Today we try to make everyone happy and glad without anyone getting mad. I challenge you – are you preaching the same message that your Saviour preached, the same that the early Church preached and for which it suffered great persecutions? Rather than causing some stirrings and commotions in the city like Elijah, we are enjoying and basking in popularity! Preachers be informed – popularity with men is never a sign of approval with God. In fact it might be the exact opposite.

We must go back to preaching the basics, not feeding the materialistic cravings of the people. Today we have too many instant believers, because we have given them a misguided message that God is an instant God. Remember the patriarchs received the promise after they had patiently waited for the promise.

> *'We do not want you to become lazy, but to imitate those who through faith and patience inherit what has been promised.'*　　　　　　　　　　　(Hebrews 6:12)

I believe that in spite of the pathetic moral and spiritual state of the majority of churches in Britain, God still desires to turn things around – to awaken the sleeping Church, send the rain of revival, and breakthrough, using the Church to transform this society. However, before this can happen it is crucial that we acknowledge our need of God, turn to Him in prayer and ask Him to heal our land. The cry of the Church in Britain at this hour should be:

> 'Blow the trumpet in Zion,
>   declare a holy fast,
>   call a sacred assembly . . .
> Let the priests, who minister before the LORD,
>   weep between the temple porch and the altar.
> Let them say, "Spare your people, O LORD." '
>
> (Joel 2:15, 17a)

As we wait on the Lord to do a sovereign work in His Church, we join Graham Kendrick and Chris Rollinson singing:

> Restore, O Lord
> The honour of Your name,
> In works of sov'reign power
> Come shake the earth again,
> That men may see
> And come with reverent fear
> To the living God
> Whose kingdom shall outlast the years.
>
> Restore, O Lord,
> In all the earth Your fame,
> And in our time revive
> The church that bears Your name.
> And in Your anger,
> Lord, remember mercy,
> O living God
> Whose mercy shall outlast the years.

Bend us, O Lord,
Where we are hard and cold,
In Your refiner's fire
Come purify the gold.
Though suffering comes
And evil crouches near,
Still our living God
Is reigning, He is reigning here.

Restore, O Lord
The honour of Your name,
In works of sov'reign power
Come shake the earth again,
That men may see
And come with reverent fear
To the living God
Whose kingdom shall outlast the years.

(Thankyou Music, Eastbourne, UK)

Chapter 7

Divine Judgement –
Any Lessons for Us Today?

'Now we know that God's judgement against those who do such things is based on truth.'   (Romans 2:2a)

'Consider therefore the kindness and sternness of God: sternness to those who fell, but kindness to you ... Otherwise, you also will be cut off.'   (Romans 11:22)

'... For the LORD is a God of justice.
  Blessed are all who wait for Him!'   (Isaiah 30:18b)

'... surely there is a God who judges the earth.'
                                                (Psalm 58:11)

'Now these things occurred as examples to keep us from setting our hearts on evil things as they did.'
                                        (1 Corinthians 10:6)

The Bible speaks quite extensively about the nature and character of the Christian God. By this we mean the properties or qualities of the Divine Being. Theologians are generally agreed on a number of attributes of God as having been revealed in Scripture. They include infinity, eternity, immutability, self-sufficiency, omnipotence, omnipresence, omniscience, truth, love, mercy, grace and of course justice. Both the Old and the New Testaments portray God as a God of justice.

The justice of God embodies the idea of moral equity. It could also be seen as God's holiness as manifested and applied in moral government. Thus when God judges, what He is simply doing is applying equity to moral situations and this may be favourable or unfavourable according to whether the person or group of persons under examination have been equitable or inequitable in heart and conduct.

So what can we learn about divine judgements from God's Holy Book? After all, history functions both to inform us about our past as well as to point us to the direction where things are heading. History instructs or teaches us about the lessons of life: why things happened the way they did and the effects they had. Thus with information about the past, the historian can almost certainly predict the future.

The Bible itself challenges us to learn from history, so that we may not only be better equipped for how to live our lives, but more importantly so that we may not repeat history. Twice, Paul the apostle challenges the Corinthian Christians to learn from history. He charges them to learn from the lives of those who had lived evil and sinful lives and the consequences of their lives.

> 'Now these things occurred as examples to keep us from setting our hearts on evil things as they did.'
>
> (1 Corinthians 10:6)

Again in verse 11 of the same chapter he remarks,

> 'These things happened to them as examples and were written down as warnings for us . . . '

The prophet Jeremiah in the same vein was instructed by God to warn wicked Israel to learn from history.

> *'Go now to the place in Shiloh where I first made a dwelling for my Name, and see what I did to it because of the wickedness of my people Israel.'* (Jeremiah 7:12)

Shiloh had been the place where the temple of God had been built. It was the place where the whole nation gathered to meet with their God. However Israel's spiritual leaders and the whole nation had fallen into iniquity. Because of this God judged the nation. Before God's judgement fell, it was preceded by warnings, but they fell on deaf ears. What was the consequence of God's judgement on Israel? The high priest and his children all died on the same day! The nation was defeated and destroyed by the enemy and the ark of God was captured. All this happened because the nation was living in sin. Many years after this, God was now telling Israel to look back into history and see the folly and consequences of breaking God's law. Perhaps they might learn from history and make amendments. Did they? No. As Scripture reveals to us – Israel was later on taken into captivity by Babylon and their magnificent temple was destroyed.

Sodom and Gomorrah

Again, another story where we can learn about God's judgement in the past is the destruction of Sodom and Gomorrah. As pointed out in the last chapter, Ezekiel 16:49–50 highlights the reasons for their destruction, including pride, thoughtless ease and detestable things. My submission then and now is that one of the reasons why they came under divine judgement was because of their homosexual practices. As Genesis chapter 19 reveals, when the men of the city came into Lot's house they demanded to have sexual relations with his visitors and even when he tried offering them his two daughters they declined and insisted on having unnatural sex with the men. So what was God's verdict on these twin cities? He overthrew their cities and destroyed everyone by raining down burning sulphur and fire!

> '... he [God] *condemned the cities of Sodom and Gomorrah by burning them to ashes, and made them an example of what is going to happen to the ungodly ...*'
>
> (2 Peter 2:6)

Judgement on the antediluvian age (the generation of Noah)

What about the antediluvian age? Any lessons to learn? The antediluvian age belonged to the generation of Noah. What were their sins? They were guilty of breaking down the divinely established order of created beings. They also practised experimentation across species. Like Sodom and Gomorrah, they incurred divine displeasure meted out through extermination. Genesis 6 records the generation's depravity and the divine response.

> 'The LORD *saw how great man's wickedness on the earth had become, and that every inclination of the thoughts of his heart was only evil all the time. The* LORD *was grieved that he had made man on the earth, and his heart was filled with pain. So the* LORD *said, "I will wipe mankind, whom I have created, from the face of the earth ... "'*
>
> (Genesis 6:5–7)

The Bible is littered with other examples of divine judgement meted out to those who chose to break God's righteous laws.

The judgement of Lucifer

Lucifer was kicked out of heaven for rebelling against God's authority. Scripture records,

> *'How you are fallen from heaven,*
> *O morning star, son of the dawn!*
> *You have been cast down to the earth,*
> *you who once laid low the nations!*
> *You said in your heart,*
> *"I will ascend to heaven;*
> *I will raise my throne*
> *above the stars of God;*
> *I will sit enthroned on the mount of assembly,*
> *on the utmost heights of the sacred mountain.*
> *I will ascend above the tops of the clouds;*
> *I will make myself like the Most High."*
> *But you are brought down to the grave,*
> *to the depths of the pit.'* (Isaiah 14:12–15)

Divine judgement on a Christian couple

In the New Testament, Ananias and Sapphira, a Christian couple, had judgement executed upon them because of their sins of deception and dishonesty recorded in Acts 5:1–11.

> *'Now a man named Ananias, together with his wife Sapphira, also sold a piece of property. With his wife's full knowledge he kept back part of the money for himself, but brought the rest and put it at the apostles' feet.*
>
> *Then Peter said, "Ananias, how is it that Satan has so filled your heart that you have lied to the Holy Spirit and have kept for yourself some of the money you received for the land? Didn't it belong to you before it was sold? And after it was sold, wasn't the money at your disposal? What*

made you think of doing such a thing? You have not lied to men but to God."

When Ananias heard this, he fell down and died. And great fear seized all who heard what had happened. Then the young men came forward, wrapped up his body, and carried him out and buried him.

About three hours later his wife came in, not knowing what had happened. Peter asked her, "Tell me, is this the price you and Ananias got for the land?"

"Yes," she said, "that is the price."

Peter said to her, "How could you agree to test the Spirit of the Lord? Look! The feet of the men who buried your husband are at the door, and they will carry you out also."

At that moment she fell down at his feet and died. Then the young men came in and, finding her dead, carried her out and buried her beside her husband. Great fear seized the whole church and all who heard about these events.'

Judgement on King Herod

Again in Acts 12:19b–23, we read another account of the early Church, where a man of high political ranking, King Herod, came under divine judgement because of pride and arrogance. He tried to take for himself the glory that belonged to God. Here is the account of the story.

'Then Herod went from Judea to Caesarea and stayed there a while. He had been quarrelling with the people of Tyre and Sidon; they now joined together and sought an audience with him. Having secured the support of Blastus, a trusted personal servant of the king, they asked for peace, because they depended on the king's country for their food supply.

On the appointed day Herod, wearing his royal robes, sat on his throne and delivered a public address to the people. They shouted, "This is the voice of a god, not of a man." Immediately, because Herod did not give praise to God, an angel of the Lord struck him down, and he was eaten by worms and died.'

Notice with me that it was the angel of the Lord that struck him down. God was responsible for his judgement, because he tried to take the glory that belonged to God. Another important thing that I want to draw your attention to is the fact that the two examples I have just cited are from the New Testament. There are too many people in the western world today who seem to hold the view that the God of the New Testament is simply the God of grace and mercy. They cannot think of the God of the New Testament age as the God who judges, after all no loving father will ever want any evil to befall his children. This is a distorted view of God. I suspect this is a manifestation of our materialistic craving that tries to live our lives with little or no reference to God, yet cling on to the pleasures and enjoyments of this passing age; and yet we want to fall into the delusion that God will not bring judgement to lives lived without reference to God. Too many Christian leaders in the west today do not have a theology of divine judgement. I have often raised the idea of Britain facing the possibility of divine judgement for neglecting God's ways and turning against Him. One would think that if anyone would understand this they would be Christian leaders, but far be it from them. Some react strongly at the thought of this possibility.

We need a balanced theology

I believe there are too many preachers who are motivated by material gain, preachers who have rushed for profit into Balaam's error. They are shepherds who feed only themselves, men who are reprobates as far as the gospel is concerned. They have done much more damage to the cause of Christ than anyone can imagine. They have led many astray, preaching peace and prosperity when the law of God has been trampled under their feet!

If there was a time that we need a balanced message it is now. After all we are charged to rightly divide the word of truth. We are to preach the total counsel of God, and this includes all the divine attributes including justice!

I must reiterate that I believe in the God of grace. I believe in the God of love. I believe in the God of mercy. These are divine attributes that we must not only believe, but they must be preached with all vigour if we are not going to fall into the error of legalism. Too many people only see God as a policeman, seated very high in heaven with a big stick waiting for us to make the slightest mistake and thus mete out our due punishment.

This view does not issue forth from a reverential fear of God. Our love and actions for God in this case will be motivated out of fear rather than love. This is not the picture that the Bible paints. God is a God of love, He's a God of grace – the God of the second chance, third, fourth, fifth, etc. God longs to bless and forgive us, much more than He's ever willing to judge us. The Bible again and again says He's not willing that any should perish: cf 2 Peter 3:9; 1 Timothy 2:4; John 3:16–17.

However, there is the other side of God. His holiness and love demands that He also judges. We all are conversant with the idea of justice. Can you imagine a world without justice, where people can do whatever they like – kill, maim, steal, disrupt the peace of society, yet go scot free? This would not be the kind of society that you or anyone would like to live in. God's love demands that He judges and chastises His children. These two are never in opposition to one another. I have not seen a parent who genuinely loves his children, yet he sees them go astray without warning and, if not heeded, exercising discipline. I am a father of two children. I love my children dearly. I want the best for them in life. I want them to be morally upright, disciplined, honourable people who fear God. However, I would be a bad parent if I saw my children going astray and yet I did not warn them and if need be discipline them.

When I discipline my children, it is usually motivated out of love. I want them to be better individuals. I do not just discipline them for the sake of disciplining. It also has a redemptive and restorative purpose. The same applies to God. Whenever God exercises justice it is usually out of love, and it is meant to redeem and restore us back to the path of righteousness. It is with this background that I seek to be understood.

I wonder what kind of Bible people read when they dismiss divine justice as a thing of the past? I wonder what kind of God they serve? You cannot read both the Old and the New Testaments and not come to an unreserved conclusion that the God of the Bible is a God of justice.

Divine judgements in contemporary times

So does God still exercise judgement on earth today or is divine judgement a thing of the past? Surely all that the Bible claims to be divine judgement cannot be such for a modern mind, which tends to prefer natural explanations for any events that were considered acts of divine judgement some centuries ago?

I am a firm believer in the fact that God is still very active in the affairs of men today, just as much as He was many centuries ago. I don't believe in the absentee God, who just finished the work of creation and thereafter escaped to an unknown destination without having anything to do with His creation. I believe in the God who is the Governor among the nations. I believe in the God that does not change. About His nature, He declares in the Bible:

> *'I the* LORD *do not change ... '* (Malachi 3:6)

Again,

> *'Jesus Christ is the same yesterday and today, and forever.'* (Hebrews 13:8)

Notice the God of the Bible does not change, He's the same forever. He will act the same way that He acted in the Bible. If He exercised justice in Bible times, we must expect the same in our times. Times may change, man may change, but never God. He never changes His ways or standards.

So are there acts that we can point to today as acts of divine judgements? I think so. Let's consider a few.

The Nigerian story

I was born in the nation of Nigeria. Nigeria by the grace of God is a nation that is richly endowed both with natural and human resources. For many decades now, the nation has not only depended on crude oil as the mainstay of the economy, but this has brought enormous wealth to the nation. So buoyant was the Nigerian economy in the

1970s that the Nigerian Naira became very strong, almost at a par with the British pound. Would Nigerians be thankful to God for this buoyant economy? Would it cause them to worship, reverence and honour Him? Would they exalt righteousness and hate iniquity? Would they care for the socially disadvantaged and marginalised?

One would think so. This was not to be the case. Rather than worship the true and living God and care for one another, the nation became engrossed in immoral and riotous living. Idolatry was rife in the country. It was very common for a man to be married and yet have concubines as well. Many only served God with their lips. Most of the traditional churches had a monument rather than a movement. Belonging to the secret societies and cults became the fad. In this state of moral and spiritual decadence, God sent one prophet after the other – warning the nation of dire consequences if she refused to repent of her wicked ways, turn to God and exalt right-eousness. As a young man I can vividly remember at least one of these prophets who called the nation to repent-ance, and pointed at the iniquity of the government. Would the nation heed the warnings of God? Would they budge? Far from it. The people were too much caught up in riotous living. The economy seemed to be impregnable. Everything seemed to be going well.

However, Nigeria was to suffer severe consequences for neglecting God's warning. For, from 1979 God permitted military and political leaders to rule Nigeria; their wicked reign can only be likened to that of Nero. So wicked and heartless were these leaders that they misappropriated, embezzled and looted the national treasury, so that a nation that was once the pride of Africa became one of the poorest nations on earth. So heartless were the leaders that once a key minister of government was interviewed about the serious state of the citizens and he remarked that things were not that bad. At least people were not picking food from the dustbin. Indeed, the minister seemed then to be prophesying. Things grew so much worse that a high percentage of Nigerians earned their living by picking things from the rubbish bins.

Today everyone is pointing to the revival of Christianity in Nigeria, such that recently the nation produced the first born-again president in its forty years as a nation. We have seen several hundreds if not thousands of church plants by people raised in the nation. We have witnessed single gatherings that have had over a million people. At the moment, if we look around we will see that believers who have been raised in the nation of Nigeria are not only involved in ministry work in almost every corner of Great Britain but, by the grace of God, they are leading some of the strongest ministries in this land.

How has this come about? It has not been cheap or easy. Revival in Nigeria has been born out of suffering and affliction. For over two-and-a-half decades, spanning four wicked political and military leaders, the pride of the nation, the economy, was mismanaged and looted and this led to an unprecedented suffering among the citizens.

Many qualified professionals lost their jobs, civil servants went without pay often for six months, and more patients died prematurely because there weren't essential drugs; many people fled the country for Europe and America, for greener pastures, and some of them are people that are leading vibrant churches in the United Kingdom. Revival in Nigeria was born, not out of prosperity, but out of adversity, suffering and affliction, because the nation refused to heed God's warning in the days of its prosperity.

The destruction of London 1665–66

Since my message is to the nation of Britain, it is necessary to take us back to our history. David Wilkerson, one of America's prophetic voices today, has done good research on the famous Great Fire of London of 1666. He writes in his book *America's Last Call* (Wilkerson Trust Publication, 1998, pp. 79–84):

'There is an instructive lesson to us in what God brought down on London in 1665–66. At that time, London was the world's most prosperous city.'

He goes on to describe London:

'London was also known as the business mart of the world. Its ships sailed the oceans, bringing home the wealth of all nations. Moreover, London was filled with stately churches, magnificent public buildings, kings' palaces, great monuments. And it was considered a Christian city, a center for religious activities. A number of great men of God preached in London at the time, and the city was populated by many praying believers.

But London's wealth and prosperity began to corrupt its multitudes. There was a high rate of employment, an abundance of wealth and the finest of materials and goods. And soon people began to indulge their fleshly lusts, wallowing in drinking and feasting. Atheism and agnosticism became acceptable and even popular philosophies of life. Fornication became common-place, and prostitution grew rampant. Large areas of the city became impoverished, and the poor were neglected and despised.

Many Christians were grieved as this spirit of iniquity fell over London. Great men of God – preachers such as Richard Baxter and John Owen – cried out warnings from the scriptures: *'I spake unto thee in thy prosperity; but thou saidst, I will not hear...'* (Jeremiah 22:21). These men delivered dire messages to the English population that were so powerful, I shudder as I read them today. They warned of coming judgments, pestilences, the collapse of businesses, fires falling on the city. Some of their messages were so scathing, so piercing, I could never imagine preaching them!

Yet their warnings fell on deaf ears. London simply refused to hear. The people said, "How can the most prosperous city on earth suddenly fall to devastation, fire, pestilence?" But in 1665, a plague of smallpox suddenly engulfed London. In just a few months, thousands of people died. The stench of death quickly filled the city, and those who could fled to safer places. Bodies were piled on wooden carts and the poor were buried in mass graves. The pestilence had come as prophesied!

Finally, near the end of that year, the plague was stayed. As 1666 dawned, the crisis seemed to have passed. Yet, did London sit up and take notice? Did the people see God's hand of warning in it all? No! The city immediately reverted to its wicked ways. Now everyone thought they could survive any crisis. London was impregnable, infallible – and their prosperity would last forever! According to English records, the city was 2,770 years old at the time. So some people reasoned, "Jerusalem stood 1,179 years.

But we've survived a thousand years longer. How can a city that has existed almost 3,000 years be destroyed?"

Then, on Sunday, September 2, 1666 – at 2 a.m., while London slept – a madman named Hubert set fire to a house on Pudding Lane. Within hours, the fire spread uncontrollably. There had been no rain in London for weeks, and the houses and buildings went up like dry tinder. The night became a blaze of fire and smoke, and people ran through the streets screaming in terror.

There are several written accounts of this infamous burning of the city of London. These accounts describe a raging fire no one could extinguish, spreading throughout the city and consuming everything in four days of sheer holocaust. Eighty-four churches were burned to the ground. Monuments melted down to nothing. Mansions were decimated. Thousands upon thousands of buildings were laid to waste, the city's whole infrastructure was destroyed.

Overnight, the wealthy became paupers. During the fire, they had run into the streets with their precious possessions, yelling, "Forty pounds for a cart!" They were offering what amounted to several hundred dollars just to be able to haul their valuables to safety. But it was to no avail – they escaped only with their lives! Their fine art, jewelry, estate papers, furs, clothes, silverware, crystal – all were destroyed. Here is a firsthand account by a writer of that time:

"Oh, the sad looks, the pale cheeks, the weeping eyes, the smiting of breasts, the wringing of hands that was to be seen in every street and on every corner. What a consternation did my eyes behold upon the minds of all men in that day of the Lord's wrath! There is no expressing of the sighs, the tears, the fears, the frights, and the amazement of the citizens, who were now compassed about with flames of fire. Many rich men, that had enough time to have removed their goods, their wares, flattered themselves that the fires would not reach their habitations. They thought they were safe and secure. But they did not escape."

John Owen, the Puritan, wrote:

"Ah, London, London! How long has the Lord been striving with thee by his Spirit, by his word, by his messengers, by his mercies, and by lesser judgements, and yet thou hast been incorrigible, incurable, and irrecoverable under all! God looked that the agues, fevers, smallpox, strange sickness, want of trade, and poverty that was coming on like an armed man upon thee, with all the lesser fires that have been kindled in the midst of thee, should have awakened thee to repentance; and yet under all, how proud, how stout, how hard, how obdurate hast thou been!

God looked that the bloody sword that the nations round hath drawn against thee should have humbled thee, and brought thee to his foot: and yet thou hast rejected the remedy of thy recovery. God looked that the raging, devouring pestilence [smallpox] that in 1665 destroyed so many ten thousands of thy inhabitants should have astonished thee, and have been as a prodigy unto thee, to have affrighted thee but of thy sins, and to have turned thee to the Most High:

But yet after so stupendous and amazing judgements, thou wast hardened in thy sins, and refusedst to return. By all these divers kinds of judgements, how little did God prevail with thy magistracy, ministry, or commonality to break off their sins, to repent, and to abhor themselves in dust and ashes! Hath not God spent all his rods in vain upon thee?...

When after the raging pestilence men returned to the city, and to their estates and trades ... they returned also to their old sins; and as many followed the world more greedily than ever, so many followed their lusts, their sinful courses, more violently than ever; and this has ushered in thy desolation, O London! ... How many within and without thy walls did make their belly their god, their kitchen their religion, their dresser their altar, and their cook their minister, whose whole felicity did lie in eating and drinking, whose bodies were as sponges, and whose throats were as open sepulchres to take in all precious liquors, and whose bellies were as graves to bury all God's creatures in!"

After the burning of London, the knight Sir Edward Turner gave a speech to the king at the convening of Parliament. He said:

"We must forever with humility acknowledge the justice of God in punishing this whole nation by the late dreadful conflagration of London. We know they were not the greatest sinners on whom the tower of Siloam fell and doubtless all our sins did contribute to the filling up of that measure, which being full, drew down the wrath of God upon that city..."

The king responded to Turner's speech with a repentant attitude:

> "His majesty therefore, out of a deep and pious sense of what himself and all his people now suffer, and with a religious care to prevent what may yet be feared, unless it shall please Almighty God to turn away his anger from us, doth hereby publish and declare his royal will and pleasure, that Wednesday, being the tenth of October next ensuing, shall be set apart, and kept, and observed by all his majesty's subjects of England and Wales ... as a day of solemn fasting and humiliation, to implore the mercies of God, that it would please him to pardon the crying sins of this nation, those especially which have drawn down this last and heavy judgement upon us, and to remove from us all his other judgments which our sins have deserved, and which we now either feel or fear...
>
> Not only the blessed Scriptures, but also king and Parliament, do roundly conclude that it was for our sins, our manifold iniquities, our crying sins, that God has sent this heavy judgement upon us."

London was slowly rebuilt. But it never regained its glory as the center of international commerce!'

(America's Last Call, David Wilkerson 1998)

As an historian, the first thing that struck my attention was the similarities between 17th-century London and that of the 21st century. The socio-political, economic, moral and spiritual climate seems to fit perfectly with what obtains today. So similar are we today that I am beginning to wonder whether we are not on course to repeat history. Are we going to learn from our own past or are we going to harden our hearts like the Londoners of the 17th century and invite divine judgement? Let us remember the wise words of the famous US philosopher George Santayana, who said,

> 'Those who do not learn from the past [history] are condemned to repeat it.'
> (*Who Said What*, Chancellor Press, 1993, London)

Another important thing worth mentioning about these judgements is the response by the political leaders of the day. We have seen how Sir Edward Turner gave a speech to the king at the convening of parliament. 'We must forever with humility acknowledge the justice of God in punishing this whole nation by the late dreadful conflagration of London...' Remember these were the words of no mean person! He was one of the movers and shakers of his days.

If Sir Edward Turner's remark does not get our attention today – maybe that of the king might! Not only did the king believe and affirm that the infamous 1666 fire came as a judgement upon the nation, but he declared a day set apart for prayer, fasting and national mourning and repentance. Oh that her majesty Queen Elizabeth II, would follow in this godly step and lead this nation on a similar path. Oh that Tony Blair and his cabinet would read this! Oh that the Church of Christ in this nation may lead this nation back to God in national repentance.

Whither Britannia?

So where is Britain heading today? How close could we be to anything like the 1665–66 pestilence and fire? I am not a prophet, nor have I been sent to give prophetic declarations as 'thus says the Lord', but I believe I am at liberty to speak as a man that has the Spirit of the Lord. I believe God has been giving this nation warning signals about what might lie ahead. I believe the handwriting is so clear on the wall for those who will take notice.

I came across an interesting article on the front page of the *Daily Telegraph* of Tuesday, 31 October 2000 captioned 'Divine Displeasure?'! My reaction to this article was: the editor without doubt must have been inspired by God. For he raises issues that any sincere and serious minded person in this nation will take to heart in his article. He writes:

> 'Not many centuries ago, pretty well everybody in these islands would have agreed that if the River Uck burst its banks or high winds lashed the coast from Cornwall to Kent, there could be only one explanation: God was angry.
>
> Today we are more sophisticated than that. We look for other causes of unusual weather conditions and the suffering and inconvenience that they cause. Meteorologists cite areas of high and low pressure, cyclones and anti-cyclones. Ecologists (the heirs of the religious zealots of earlier times) ascribe the floods to "global warming" – although, as Matt Ridley points out opposite, there is no proven basis for their warnings that weather patterns are changing.
>
> Perhaps we have been too quick to dismiss the simple certainties of our forebears. God after all must find an awful lot to be angry about when he casts his all seeing eye over Cool Britannia. Look at the sequence of events: on Friday, the Archbishop of Canterbury announces that modern Britons are a bunch of atheists; the very next day, the heavens

open over his cathedral and plunge the people of Kent up to their knees in water. Coincidence, eh? When the winds howl over Bognor, might not the Almighty be commenting on Parliament's decision to lower the age of homosexual consent? Or the abortion rate? Or the breakdown of marriage? Or the sheer greed and selfishness of so many Britons these days? These explanations are at least as plausible as the theory of global warming.'

Could God be speaking to us today?

To this I say a big yes! I believe that in the final quarter of the year 2000, the fuel and rail crisis could also be warning signs for this country. I believe God has been using these signs to draw our attention to Him, to warn this nation of the five million innocent babies that have been aborted through state laws, for the high tide of sexual perversion and promiscuity, for the compromise in the Church.

Sodom did not have gay activitists, yet it perished! Sodom did not have priests – supposed representatives of God – trying to change their sex, yet it perished. I have often said that unless Great Britain repents of its grave iniquity, God might have to apologise to the people of Sodom and Gomorrah.

So how close are we to a possible divine judgement? I have a feeling that, unless there is national repentance led by Christians, a heartfelt sorrow for our wicked ways and sins, if things continue the way they are today – Great Britain will be on a collision course with God. I believe so great will be the impact of whatever God chooses to do that it will get the attention of everyone – both the government and the governed, the rich and the poor, the citizens and the visitors. I suspect that God may break the pride of Britain – our economy.

But it doesn't have to be so, for He promised that,

> *'If my people, who are called by my name, will humble themselves and pray and seek my face and turn from their wicked ways, then will I hear from heaven and will forgive their sin and will heal their land.'*   (2 Chronicles 7:14)

Chapter 8

Repentance

'Or do you show contempt for the riches of his kindness, tolerance and patience, not realising that God's kindness leads you towards repentance?'   (Romans 2:4)

'He is patient with you, not wanting anyone to perish, but everyone to come to repentance.'   (2 Peter 3:9b)

We have seen so far that Britain had very early contact with Christianity. Her laws, political machinery and education system were all built on Christian foundations. Britain from its earliest beginnings entered into a spiritual covenant through the Coronation Oath with the true and living God. Britain has enjoyed great revivals and awakenings that have not only transformed this nation but have been imparted to many nations abroad. In all this God has been at work. We are told in Ephesians 1:11 that God works out everything in conformity with the purpose of His will.

As a result of embracing the Christian gospel, Britain not only acknowledged God again and again in its national life, but God in return blessed her with a good economy and gave her one of the largest empires the world has known in modern history. She also became

God's voice to the nations, the number one missionary-sending nation. We have also seen that Britain has unfortunately been overtaken by national pride like Israel. Britain, like Jeshurun, is full, has waxed strong, and has kicked against the rock of His salvation and the holy one of Israel that made her great. Today not only has God been sidelined in our land, but now we are on a collision course with God.

Britain is filled with iniquity and abomination. The spiritual leaders who are supposed to lead the nation in the paths of righteousness are blind guides. There is great sin in God's camp today. Abominations are occurring among the people that profess to know God as well as outside the Church. The abomination in this land at the moment has reached such unimaginable proportions that it is the opinion of the author that unless a drastic change occurs Britain is likely to experience divine judgement that might reach catastrophic proportions.

When I started writing this book Britain was in the midst of an outbreak of **foot and mouth disease**. As it goes to press **bovine tuberculosis** has just broken out in cattle in Wales. I believe these are examples of divine judgement.

Consider this for a moment! In 1967 Britain passed the state murder law, called 'The Abortion Act' – this was followed by an outbreak of **foot and mouth disease**. In 2001 the government permitted the sale of the morning after pill over the counter – another convenient way of promoting the destruction of innocent lives. The government also passed a bill to experiment with human embryos through cloning. Guess what followed these two bills toying with human lives? **foot and mouth disease**.

I believe that Britain has crossed the line of God's grace and unless there is a change in people's way of living, our attitude, we will face a terrible judgement that will get everyone's attention. I believe in divine judgement and I do not pretend to hide this. When Britain lived according to the laws of God, we didn't have as much material prosperity, yet we had far more stable family relationships. Marriages lasted longer, children were taught values, they honoured their parents and the elderly. Our society was much safer. People cared more for their neighbours. Indeed, they were their neighbour's keeper. However, things have changed today. The crime and abortion rates have reached unimaginable proportions. Pornography has become a major British industry destroying many lives and marriages. Today we have almost one million children who have never seen their father due to family breakdown. At the moment Britain is in crisis, Britain is a sick society. She is in urgent need of healing. Britain's sickness is critical, but not hopeless. Only one thing can save Britain from destruction – **repentance**. Repentance means a fundamental and thorough change in the hearts of men from sin against God. It means changing our attitudes and lifestyles. It means having an afterthought. It means forsaking our evil ways and now pursuing good. It means making amends where we have erred. We read in the Bible the story of the prodigal son who left his father and went about living a riotous life. However, after a while he came back to his senses; in other words he repented, had a change of mind and thereafter returned to his father and asked for forgiveness. Just as the prodigal son, we have gone away from our Father (God), and today we are living without any recourse to Him or His ways. We must go back and ask Him for pardon.

God is never interested in our destruction. He is interested in our salvation, in our good. Sin does destroy, but God does not want us to be destroyed.

In 2 Peter 3:9, we are told that,

> *'The Lord is not slow in keeping his promise, as some understand slowness. He is patient with you, not wanting anyone to perish, but everyone to come to repentance.'*

God does not want anyone to perish. He does not want a single soul to be destroyed. Rather He wants them to turn to Him in repentance and to have a change of heart. I believe that the main reason why God told me to write this book is to challenge us to turn from our wicked ways to Him. I believe God is giving Britain another chance to repent. The reason why God is sending many of His servants to us is not to condemn us, but to plead with us – so that we can turn to Him. I believe God is more interested in showing mercy than in executing judgement. He's calling out to us today because He does not want to exercise judgement. I believe the Father heart of God for this nation at the moment is reflected in the book of Hosea chapter 11 verse 8, where He shows His reluctance to execute judgement on Israel. Listen to the pleading of a loving father,

> *'How can I give you up, Ephraim?*
> *How can I hand you over, Israel?*
> *How can I treat you like Admah?*
> *How can I make you like Zeboiim?*
> *My heart is changed within me;*
> *all my compassion is aroused.'*

This pleading is in spite of the fact that Israel has forsaken Him, gone after idols and has lived sinfully.

If ever there was a time that we needed to go back to God with a broken, repentant heart, it is now. If we do we can be sure that He will not turn us away, but rather heal us. Let's receive some instructions from the prophet Hosea.

> 'Come, let us return to the LORD.
>   He has torn us to pieces
>   but he will heal us;
> he has injured us
>   but he will bind up our wounds.
> After two days he will revive us;
>   on the third day he will restore us,
>   that we may live in his presence.
> Let us acknowledge the LORD,
>   let us press on to acknowledge him.
> As surely as the sun rises,
>   he will appear;
> he will come to us like the winter rains,
>   like the spring rains that water the earth.'

(Hosea 6:1–3)

The foot and mouth epidemic has had such uncontrollable proportions that it not only paralysed whole industries, but it has been exported to Europe. Could this be a coincidence? Could it be a judgement from God? I leave you to judge!

We have done it before!

Individual and mass repentance is not something that is foreign to us in Great Britain. Our history is littered with times in which whole towns, cities and indeed the nation were led in national prayer and repentance. At times the instruments that God used were spiritual leaders. At other times they were led by our political leaders. It happened during the Great Awakening led by George Whitefield and John Wesley. It happened more than once in the various Welsh revivals.

We have seen earlier in this book how our political leaders responded to the famous London fire of 1666. After the burning of London, the Knight Sir Edward Turner gave a speech to the king at the convening of Parliament. He said 'We must forever with humility acknowledge the justice of God in punishing this whole nation by the late dreadful conflagration of London' (David Wilkerson, *America's Last Call*, Wilkerson Trust Publication, 1998, p. 83).

I salute the manner in which the king responded to Turner's speech and afterwards declared a day of national prayer of repentance and fasting for all the subjects of England and Wales. He remarked, that 'Not only the blessed scriptures, but also king and parliament, do roundly conclude that it was for our sins, our manifold iniquities, our crying sins, that God has sent this heavy judgement upon us' (David Wilkerson, *America's Last Call*, p. 84).

During the last war God-fearing leaders, especially our sovereign King George VI, called this nation to prayer – to ask for help and mercy from God. And God indeed answered our prayers and this was acknowledged nationally. Even our major newspapers covered this. I pray that our Queen would follow in the godly steps of her father and lead this nation in a day or in seasons of national repentance, for mercy to be shown to this backslidden land.

It's happening in other cities and nations

Cali in Colombia used to be a notorious place for drug trafficking. Many drug barons made much money from this illegal trade. As would be expected, the trade in drugs brought with it so much evil, such as violence, murder, sexual promiscuity, etc. The moral and spiritual state in Cali was so alarming that a pastors' fraternity was formed to pray and seek God on behalf of their city. Even though they lost the chief architect of this revival through daylight murder, Cali was, however, to experience the transforming power of God such that the whole fabric of society has now been totally transformed – from the mayor of the city, to celebrities in sports and music and the man on the street. How did this transformation come about? The spiritual leaders in the city began to meet and confess the sins of their city and the Church to God. Whole nights they filled the city stadium for prayer and intercession. What was the outcome? God heard from heaven, forgave their sins and healed the land. Now Cali is one of the key spots of revival in South America.

Nigeria is experiencing great spiritual awakening at the moment, such that as recently as the beginning of 2001 the evangelist Reinhard Bonnke held a week-long evangelistic crusade in Lagos and about 1.6 million people were reported to have made first-time decisions for Christ. How has this come about? As mentioned earlier in this book, the revival in Nigeria and many other West African states has not come cheap. It has come about from the pot of affliction. People have been forced to seek God, because God withdrew their sources of comfort and pleasure.

It is not unusual for spiritual leaders to declare days, weeks and months to seek God in prayer and repentance on behalf of the nation. As recently as September 2000, the intercessors for Nigeria (led by Emeka Nwankpa) held an intercession conference. One of our illustrious and patriotic sons, Brian Mills, attended the conference. Hear his report about the conference:

'The next day I can only describe as "historic". It was their National Day of Repentance. I have never been anywhere where such a level of genuine repentance was manifested. For nine hours, without a break, leaders of the nation confessed the sins of their nation. Members of the government and various senators were present. So too were 300–400 government legislators, politicians and civil servants. Ex Government ministers, from the time of Independence until today, a leader of Industry, tribal kings, heads of military and the secret service, church leaders – each poured out a catalogue of the sins of their group, including greed, waste, watering down of products, corruption, deceit, murder, and backhanders to the practitioners of witchcraft and idolatry. They prayed to break links with ancestors, tribal customs and alliances with evil spirits. They broke covenants made with darkness and with death.

It was utterly awesome. These were no formal prayers – these were intercessors of the highest order – and the highest rank in the land – weeping or sobbing before God as they spoke their repentance with honesty and openness.'

He concludes:

'They were laying a new foundation for Nigeria, based on righteousness. They were preparing the spiritual ground as Nigeria sought to end its wandering in the wilderness, ready to enter its promised land from the 40th Anniversary of Independence on the 1st October.'

(*Mills Messenger*, November/December 2000 and January 2001 edition – a quarterly pamphlet produced by Brian Mills of Interprayer UK)

My prayer is that Britain will learn from the Nigerian situation. After all, your spiritual fathers brought us the gospel and the Bible. They also taught us how to repent from false idols and the evil way and turn to the true and living God.

Repentance or judgement?

'See, I set before you today life and prosperity, death and destruction. For I command you today to love the LORD your God, to walk in his ways, and to keep his commands, decrees and laws; then you will live and increase, and the LORD your God will bless you in the land you are entering to possess. But if your heart turns away and you are not obedient, and if you are drawn away to bow down to other gods and worship them, I declare to you this day that you will certainly be destroyed.'

(Deuteronomy 30:15–18a)

I believe Britain will either repent and experience revival or face divine judgement, divine judgement, as I have mentioned, of serious proportions that would be felt in every nook and cranny of this nation – even in the corridors of power. Recently (December 2000), the fellowship I lead, World Harvest Christian Centre, hosted a Prophetic Prayer and Fasting Conference for this nation, where we came to confess the sins of this land to God and seek His face regarding Great Britain. One clear word that came forth from this conference was that the trumpets must be sounded all over Britain. The call to repentance must be sounded at Number 10 Downing Street. It must be sounded at Buckingham Palace; it must be sounded in the House of Commons and in the House of Lords. It must be sounded on every street in this land. The trumpet of repentance must be sounded in every church; it must be sounded in every theological seminary. Warnings must be sounded at every city centre, where we have our economic base. It must be sounded in all of our schools and ivory towers; it must be sounded to the young and the aged; it must be sounded to the clergy and to the laity. Britain is in a state of emergency. The watchmen cannot afford to sleep or slumber. There is fire all across this land. The Lord has a contention with the land. There is an angel of death already hovering over this land. Only a heartfelt turning around to God will save this nation from an imminent judgement.

Whether or not this nation will repent and experience revival or face the wrath of God is something I will not speculate about, but I will leave to future historians to write about. However, I join Graham Kendrick, one of our foremost contemporary music ministers, and several saints across this land in singing:

> Lord, the light of Your love is shining
> In the midst of the darkness, shining:
> Jesus, Light of the world, shine upon us,
> Set us free by the truth You now bring us,
> Shine on me,
> Shine on me,
> Shine on me.

Shine, Jesus, shine,
Fill this land with the Father's glory;
Blaze Spirit, blaze,
Set our hearts on fire.
Flow, river, flow,
Flood the nations with grace and mercy;
Send forth Your Word,
Lord, and let there be light.

(Make Way Music 1987)

May You, Lord, shine! Shine over Great Britain. Fill this land with the Father's glory. This is our cry and prayer in Jesus name. Amen.

Suggested practical action for this chapter

1. Spend some time reading Nehemiah chapter 1 and Ezra chapter 9, and see how these two men identified with the sins of their nation in prayer. Are there some sins that you can take to God in prayer?

2. You could also join a local prayer initiative around you. In many parts of Britain today, there are groups and churches praying together for this country.

3. You could call Ashburnham Prayer Centre in East Sussex, where regular prayer initiatives are going on.

4. There are other key groups that you can contact and ask to be on their mailing list, groups like Intercessors for Britain (14 Orchard Road, Moreton, Wirral CH46 8TS) or Lydia Fellowship International (PO Box 85, Waterlooville, Hants, PO7 7QU UK).

5. You could also read some books. One that readily comes to mind is *The Sins of the Fathers* by Roger

Mitchell and Brian Mills, published by Sovereign World.

6. Our local fellowships could spend some time on Sundays to pray for this country.

Chapter 9

There Is Hope for Britain – Great Britain Shall Be Saved!

'And so all Israel will be saved, as it is written:

> *"The deliverer will come from Zion;*
> *he will turn godlessness away from Jacob." '*
>
> (Romans 11:26)

'For the earth will be filled with the knowledge
> *of the glory of the LORD,*
> *as the waters cover the sea.'*   (Habakkuk 2:14)

I believe that Great Britain will be saved! I believe that not too far in the distant future, revival will hit this nation. So great will this revival be that it will sweep through the length and breadth of this nation. It will affect people on the streets as well as those on the throne. I believe that the revival that will hit this nation will be so grand in its scale that it will not only transform this nation, but it will be such that it will affect mainland Europe and other parts of the world. I believe this revival will bring an unprecedented harvest of souls into the kingdom of God. It will awaken the missionary fervour of Great Britain. However, this time they will be missions that are devoid of colonialism or imperialism. They will be missions without exploitation.

The great awakening of the 18th century will be insignificant compared with what God is about to do. This revival will break all race, class, sex and denominational barriers that have divided the Body of Christ. No longer will the Church in Great Britain be shattered and fragmented. In this coming revival, there shall be a full expression of the one new man in the Body of Christ. We shall no longer have 'black church', neither will we have a 'white church'. A 'middle class' or 'working class' or even 'no class' church will be a thing of the past. Christ shall be all in us and all in all. For in Christ there is neither, not either.

> *'For all of you who were baptised into Christ have clothed yourselves with Christ. There is neither Jew nor Greek, slave nor free, male nor female, for you are all one in Christ Jesus.'*　　　　　　　　　(Galatians 3:27–28)

I want to reiterate again, I believe with all my heart that Great Britain is central to the end time move of God. God began the history of salvation with the call of Abraham and the nation of Israel. Even though there has been a temporary setting aside, however, Israel still occupies a central place in the consummation of things. Paul asserts that Israel shall be saved. By this I believe he was not just speaking about the whole nation, nor do I believe that this salvation will be apart from faith in the Lord Jesus Christ. I believe he was speaking of a remnant. In the same way I believe Great Britain played a significant role in spreading abroad the knowledge of Christ into many nations of the world. It is for this reason that she became the number one missionary-sending nation. I believe that the Church in Great Britain will play again a strategic role in hastening and bringing back Jesus – the King of kings and the Lord of lords.

Perhaps a more important reason why I strongly believe that Britain will experience revival and transformation is because of the honour and glory of God. God is a jealous God. He is not only jealous for His glory, but for His name. God is jealous for His name in this land, which has been defiled and desecrated. There was a time when this nation stood for God, His name, His word and His purposes among the nations. But today God's name has been defiled – not so much among heathen or Gentile nations, but among a people that once knew the Lord. Today there are worse sins and atrocities committed in Britain than in heathen nations. Some of our ways and lifestyles are so appalling that even Muslims, Hindus and Buddhists are taken aback. It is for this reason that God has determined in His heart to turn the tide, in the very place where the name of God has been defiled, among the very people that God's name has been brought to disrepute, He has determined to lift up His name again. God's name will once again be exalted in this land. Britain I believe will experience revival.

Seeds of revival

I don't believe that Britain is already in revival! What I do, however, believe is that there are seeds of revival everywhere. All you need to do is to look around. All across this nation saints of God are becoming thirsty for revival. There is a deep hunger in people's hearts to see God visit our nation again. All across cities, towns and villages, people are gathering together to seek God in prayer for this nation. Borough-wide prayer initiatives are on the increase. God is raising up strategic, apostolic, governmental churches, which are involved in high-level spiritual warfare. Churches and Christians are now being encouraged to adopt their street and local area and believe God for their salvation and transformation. The video *Transformations* by George Otis Junior has had a tremendous impact in many fellowships and among pastors' fraternities. Ministers across this land are beginning to see the futility of going solo. They are now beginning to network on a greater scale.

Have you noticed that in almost every nook and cranny of this nation, we are beginning to see missionaries from Africa, Asia and South America? Don't be alarmed and don't be jealous. It is the working of God to fulfil God's end-time plan for this nation. These agents from these nations are the harvest of the seeds that our fathers sowed when they went out to convert the heathen nations. Rather than being jealous and treating them harshly, let's accept them as God's 'apostles', sent ones, sent here by God, not to dominate, but to serve you. In my personal experience, I have seen God bring me into some strategic relationships with Christian leaders from this land. I do love and value their relationships. In fact I am bold enough to assert that no foreign missionary into this nation will adequately fulfil God's calling over their life without taking seriously the issue of marrying this land. By this I mean, in spite of all the problems and shortcomings, we must see ourselves as being one of 'them'. I believe that in the same way in which a righteous prophet, Hosea, was commanded by God to marry a harlot with all her filth, so God is also calling us at this strategic season to marry the harlot nation called Britain. Like Nehemiah we must see ourselves as being part of the problem and the solution. We must begin to identify with the land. We must see the Queen as our Queen, the Prime Minister as our Prime Minister. We must see the problems of the nation as our problems, then we will be able to minister to this nation with compassion as God would have us.

My dream for Great Britain

Perhaps my dream for Great Britain is best expressed in the song of Chris Falson, who wrote:

> We have a vision for this nation;
> We share a dream for this land.
> We join with angels in celebration,
> By faith we speak revival to this land.
>
> Where every knee shall bow and worship You,
> And every tongue confess that You are Lord;
> Give us an open heaven; anoint our prayers this day,
> And move Your sovereign hand across this nation.
> (Kingsway Music 1990)

Yes I have a vision for this nation! I share a dream for this land. I dream of a nation where the laws of God will again be the foundations of our society. I dream of the day when the majority of our parliamentarians and government officials are committed Christians. I dream of the day when our Prime Minister will be a genuine born-again believer, who will publicly acknowledge the Lordship of Jesus over this land. I dream of the day when our public offices will be filled with people who have a heart for the poor, the down trodden, the elderly, the disabled and the citizenry and are not just out for the gains of public office. I dream of the day when the Church will be the Church. I dream of that day when we shall be the salt and light in our society. I look forward to the day when a 'black church' or a 'white church' will be a thing of the past. I dream of the day when churches all across this land will be packed. I look forward to the day when pubs will become Bible study centres. I look forward to the day when families will once again be closely knitted together. I dream of the day when our elderly people will no longer be seen as burdens, ostracised in an old people's home, waiting to die, but we will take good care of them. I look forward to the day when our children and young ones will know how to respect and honour their parents and the elderly. I dream of the day when that dreadful and inhuman thing called child abuse will be a thing of the past. I dream of a revival hitting our prison system and producing great witnesses for the Lord. I dream of a National Health Service and a transportation system that will be the pride of our nation.

I dream and I see a mighty army of missionaries being raised up from across this land, moving into mainland Europe and reaching to the ends of the earth. I see the fire of revival engulfing this land. I see the glory of the Lord enveloping this land. I see a great revival coming, so great, so grand – such that nothing of its like has been seen before in this land.

As I earnestly and prayerfully await that day, my song and prayer to God would be:

> I want to serve the purpose of God
>   in my generation.

I want to serve the purpose of God
    while I am alive.
I want to give my life
    for something that will last forever,
Oh, I delight, I delight to do your will.

I want to see the kingdom of God
  in my generation.
I want to see the kingdom of God
    while I am alive.
I want to live my life
    for something that will last forever,
Oh, I delight, I delight to do your will.

What is on your heart?
Tell me what to do.
Let me know your will
    and I will follow you.
                            (Mark Altrogge, People of Destiny, 1982)

For ministry details please contact us via our website:
www.worldharvest.org.uk